WHEN GOD WHISPERS.....

Lessons Learned in my Quiet Moments

God has whispered. I have listened.
My soul has been fed.

Jeanine – listen for His whisper... "you are loved!" ♡ Susan

Susan E. Goodson

When God Whispers.....
Lessons Learned in my Quiet Moments

ISBN: 978-0-9912962-1-7

This book is dedicated to my mother, Heather E. Temple
who gave me the gift of faith.
Thank you momma.
I will always be so grateful.

Evolving is part of our growth process.
As we grow, we change.
As we change, we see life differently.
Seeing life differently, we hear with more clarity.
With more clarity, we find our courage.
With our courage, we make wiser choices.
And with wiser choices we feed our souls.

Contents

Money...Money...Money... What's up with that?

If it's true that our core beliefs are formed in our early childhood and come from our family of origin, then I am in deep trouble.

Money.....

Money was important to my family.

I didn't learn my core values concerning money by what was said. It was more subtle than that. It's what I caught by watching and listening.

The words were few but the lessons were enormous and have affected how I've lived my life surrounding the value of the dollar bill.

When my family took week long road trips to see my grandparents and we'd stop for breakfast, I wanted to order a hamburger and a milk shake. I was told that if it wasn't breakfast food, I couldn't have it. What difference did it make to my parents what I had to eat? Did it really matter if I had scrambled eggs or a sandwich with fries? I guess it did because the message

I got was if you want to have a burger and shake, then you get a job, make your own money and buy whatever you want.

Hmmm. The message for me there was clear. Money = choices. Choices = freedom. Freedom =Power. That worked for me.

So I went to work at eleven years old to gain the independence I needed to make my own choices.

What I was learning was that I could control my world by the amount of money I had. The more money, the more control and when you come from a violent and dysfunctional childhood, all you want is some sense of personal control.

I had my answer. Work hard. Make money. Feel in control and be safe.

That childhood coping skill worked then but it sure wasn't helping me now.

I couldn't trust my parents. They were unpredictable and abusive. And that idea bled over into my adult life when it came to an understanding of a loving and caring God.

Rely on God like you would your father. What? Impossible.

Ask God for what you need? Never!

Trust God's love for you? He is there to protect and take care of you. NOT!

Money was the only thing I trusted and I lived my life looking for ways to make it. Or looking for people who had it.

I didn't know until many years later that I had sold my soul for money. And that took me places that harmed my spirit and stole my joy. It influenced how I worked and why. It took my creativity and distorted my God- given gifts into a saleable commodity. Doing anything for the pure joy of it was lost, and if what I was doing wasn't good enough to sell, then I wouldn't do it.

It saddens me to write this even now.

"Do it for the fun of it." No possible way could I live that way. There was too much work to do.

If my heart followed the money then I was doomed to a life of fear and panic, until I understood that if money was my idol, there would never be any room for God.

Hebrews 13:5 Matthew 6:21 Matthew 6:21 Luke 12:15 1Timothy 6:10

The Not Enoughs

Not enough love. Not enough time. Not enough cash.

What about love? As a child, how can one measure whether you have received the love you need?

I never felt loved, nurtured or cared for emotionally by my mom and dad. It didn't matter to me as a child that they had been wounded by their own parents, and that they couldn't give what they never got. They were my parents, and it was their job to give me love.

I didn't understand the idea that they did the best they could with what they had. All I knew when I was little was that I must not be loveable or they could have found a way to love me.

Living with an alcoholic, workaholic dad and a mother who was constantly in a state of fear, life as the oldest of five was painful and I had no clue the damaging beliefs I would carry into my adult life wrapped in a beautiful suitcase called "emotional baggage."

Fifteen months after I was born, my brother was born and so began the journey of learning the idea of limited time, energy and love. If I was only six months old when my mom was pregnant again, I imagine that her attention was already turning away from me and onto the next one. And then the next one and on and on and on.

I only had my mom's love and attention for six short months and with a dad who worked long hours and often came home drunk stumbling up the stairs, I understood that, even then, there would never be enough for me. I would always need to make room for someone else. I was now headed down an empty road and was being set up to crave attention, love and more. More of anything. I was already lost in a world affected by alcoholism.

What does not enough time look like to a kid anyway? Can we go to the park? No. We don't have time.

Can you take me to the store? No, there's too much to do.

Can I go out and ride my bike? Not until your chores are done.

I get that. I understand that kids have to be responsible and learn the value of doing their part. What I'm talking about is when dinner was over and I wanted to rush from the table to go outside and catch the end of the sunshine while I peddled around on my two-wheeler and my dad saying, "On no you don't. You have dish duty."

"Ah dad, can't I do it right after I play? It's going to be dark soon." I begged.

"Nope. Get it done now."

So I would get to washing and when everything was finished, the dishes in the drainer and my hands dried, he would inspect every plate, cup, knife and fork looking for a speck of food and when he found it, he would put all the dishes in the sink and make me do them again. And again, until they were spotless.

Was it really that important to him that every dish be perfect? I don't think so. The lesson I caught from this experience was that fun wasn't allowed and there would always be something more important to do than play.

Work. Work. Work.

And the money thing…

Until I figured out what money represented for me, I could never understand the push and obsession of needing more. If money = power and I grew up having no control over anything, then it made perfect sense that my need for money was my need for control. If I could get that, then I could create a safe space for myself. And so God got eliminated from my consciousness so I could make room for what I desperately thought I had to have. Money would give me everything I needed until that wasn't enough anymore and the cycle just got deeper and the wound bigger.

As I spent quiet time with God this morning, I was reminded that there is ALWAYS enough with Him. He always has time for me whenever I need Him. He always has my back when I am scared that I am not enough in a world that screams daily, "Do more, Have more, Be more."And He loves me more than I could even imagine in my limited human understanding.

I am heading out for the 50th Mary Kay Anniversary seminar this week and will take with me the acknowledgment and reminder that I am ENOUGH for I have been made in the image and likeness of my God. I will celebrate everyone without comparing myself and my journey to theirs. I will dance in joy for having been given an opportunity to be a part of a company that emphasizes and encourages living my life with the priorities of God-first, Family-second and Career-third. And I will be grateful for journey I am on, for it has been uniquely designed just for ME.

Isaiah 43:4 1Peter 2:9 Philippians 4:13 Psalm 138:8

Willingness

As I sat in a service club meeting early on Tuesday morning at the local Panera bread, I began to hear that all too familiar voice whispering in my head.

Oh no, not again and certainly not now I thought. I'm really trying to pay attention to what's happening at this meeting. Decisions that need to be made for our local Kiwanis club and the dialogue being exchanged between board members.

I don't have time for this.

But the voice continued.

I know this voice. It's a voice I have come to appreciate and trust, but sometimes the timing is truly inconvenient.

It is the voice of the Holy Spirit speaking on God's behalf.

Today was not a good day, I was super busy and had a full plate for the remainder of the day.

But the voice was persistent.

"Buy Gayle a loaf of bread."

"What? God I'm really busy right now."

"Buy Gayle a loaf of bread," He persisted.

"You want me to buy Gayle a loaf of bread and do what with it? Hang it on her door knob in a Mary Kay bag with a sympathy card from Vons?

"Yes" was God's response.

Gayle was a good customer of mine and have become a dear friend.

She had called a couple months earlier to ask me to come by and meet her dad who had recently moved in with her so she could care for him during his final weeks of life.

Her daddy was suffering from cancer.

I was honored to be invited and went by early one morning to say hello.

He was a kind and gentle man and I was grateful to have had the opportunity to know him, even if only for a few minutes.

It wasn't too long after I met him that she called again to share her sadness about his passing and three days later I sat in Panera bread and got the inner memo to buy the bread and leave it at her doorstep.

You can only imagine how I argued with God on this. What would she think of me? I knew Gayle would definitely believe I had lost my mind, and I was dreadfully afraid of making a fool of myself. After all, I was a professional beauty consultant, not a crazy woman.

After nearly 30 minutes of a quiet and hidden dialogue I acquiesced, swallowed my fear and stopped by the counter on my way out to buy some sesame bread. I ran across the parking lot to Von's to pick up a sympathy card and headed toward Gayle's house.

I breathed a sigh of relief when I realized she wasn't home. I left the package on the door and left as quickly as I could.

It was only just a few short days later that I got a phone call from her telling me how grateful she was that I had dropped the bread off at her home.

She told me her friends had brought dinner for that night but no one brought the bread. She and her family were able to share bread over the passing of her dad simply because I was obedient.

What a gift for all of us.

Not only did I hear the voice of the Holy Spirit but I was willing to do what was asked of me.

I was given a chance to listen and then make a choice to follow the prompting of God.

I realized, at that moment, that every day I wake up I am given the opportunity to be used by God in the quietest of ways.

I am called upon to act on God's behalf and do it joyfully.

But before anything happens I must choose to be willing.

On that day I almost let the gift pass me by because of my stubborn ego.

My prayer today is that I will hear, obey and be thankful to be chosen to do God's work especially in the simple ways.

And in doing so my life and the lives of others will be enriched and God will be glorified.

John 15:9 Revelation 14:12 John 14:15 2John 1:6

Susie, Where Are You?

As I delve into this subject I know that many of you may totally get what I am trying to say and others may think I have lost my mind. In either case here goes!

I believe that we have a pure, innocent and trusting child that lives deep inside each of us. I know I do. I call her my 'Inner Child" and she is the essence of the child of God I have always been.

However, somewhere, a long time ago, I lost her and went on my merry way of growing up and leaving her behind. "Little Susie," as I call her now, has always been THAT voice of reason that worked tirelessly to prevent me from making harmful decisions. She has been the voice that would caution me on taking the step that could lead to painful consequences. She is the one who knew what was best for me in every scenario. I believe she was the voice of God.

But I didn't want to hear her. I wanted to do to her what my parents did to me along the way. I wanted to keep her quiet. I wanted her to be still and go away. I wanted to drown out her voice.

I didn't want Little Susie telling me I was making a mistake, that I wasn't taking care of myself or that I was being destructive. I wanted what I wanted when I wanted it. And no one was going to tell me otherwise.

I had been emotionally held captive my entire life by tyrant parents, and once I moved away from home, I was FREE to make my own choices and live my own life. But if all I knew was what I learned from them, how was I ever going to function in a healthy way and make wise decisions? How would I ever know how to maneuver through the chaos of life and not be hurt in the rough rapids of everyday living?

I didn't.

I didn't make wise and healthy choices.

I didn't protect myself from decisions that would wreak havoc in my life.

I didn't listen to those who wanted to give me wise counsel.

I don't know why it was so hard to ask for help. But it was.

I believed in God but didn't trust God. If I had a dad who beat and abused me, how could I possibly trust a God who you all called "Father?"

I didn't.

And I went about my day trying to suffocate the only voice that could help me reason things out at a soulful level.

Instead I told her to shut up and be quiet. I told her that she was getting in my way of having what I wanted and that she was ruining my life.

Pretty soon, Little Susie had nothing left to say. Her voice had been taken away by the adult in me who didn't have the courage to hear her loving direction. I stole her voice and she went silent.

Would I ever have the courage to speak my truth and would anyone be listening?

ABSOLUTELY, for God always hears, cares for and welcomes our voices.

Ecclesiastes 3:7 John 15:18-19 Psalm 15:1-3 Zachariah 8:16

High Risk Prayer

At church on Sunday the sermon was on High Risk Prayer.

"Ok," I thought. "What exactly is a High Risk Prayer?"

The preacher was quick to answer my thoughts.

It is a prayer that one asks to bring about a change that is so paramount to one's life, that it will never be the same. A prayer that could change your life IMMEDIATELY.

"Hmmm." I pondered. I guess that wouldn't be the prayer that's asks God for a green light so I can get home really quick so I can go to the bathroom.

Or even the prayers that seek help for my children, my family or even my business.

A high risk prayer is that prayer that one might be too afraid to pray because everything is really good right now, so why rock the boat.

The prayer looks like this:

Please God......

1. Send me.
2. Test me.

3. Why not me.
4. Challenge me.
5. Use me.
6. Search me.
7. Teach me.

Yikes. That kind of prayer takes great courage, at least it does for me.

I like my life quiet and simple. I don't particularly go running into the closet that has the word 'Change" on top of it. You know why? Because in the past when I have opened that door even a little bit, those demons that I have been so desperately trying to hold at bay want to jump out and scare me.

Does change scare you too? Like the "What if's" of life?

Having been a part of a 12 Step Program for over 18 years I looked at what the preacher was saying and compared it to what I am working on in my program.

Step 1 is about admitting I am powerless. Oh how I didn't want to go there. Me? Powerless? No way. I can make the changes I need in myself and my family to keep things moving easily and smoothly. Right? Wrong. Who am I kidding? Control over my life and circumstances is an illusion at best.

Step 2 is about acknowledging that since I cannot control anything, such as my own mouth or my desire to indulge in sugar, I need assistance and this step encourages me to ask God to help restore my sanity. Who said anything about being crazy? If I am honest with myself and step back to look at my behavior patterns, I guess I could definitely say I have my moments.

Step 3 is all about making a decision to turn my will and my life over to the care of God. Surrender. Let go. Do my part and let go of the results. That would definitely go along the lines of "Test Me."

And Step 4 is about taking a fearless and moral inventory of myself, the seemingly good and maybe not so good. Now I can totally see this has everything to do with the "Search Me" prayer.

What I am learning weekly as I fellowship with a larger community of people who believe like me is that life gets easier when shared with others. I get filled up when I go and share space with those who encourage and love me.

Whether it's a 12 step meeting, a bible study, or community church, there are many similarities.

Life was never meant to be lived alone. We were meant to be in fellowship with others.

I don't know what your belief system is or if you even have one.

Maybe you believe in God but don't trust God. I lived in that place for most of my life. Maybe you have a Higher Power that is a force of nature like the ocean or a tree. Maybe you just talk out loud to the universe and know that something bigger than you is running the show.

What I know for me is that I hunger to be the best person I can be every day. My desire is to have God show me the character defects that keep getting in the way of me having a life of peace and serenity. I don't want to keep repeating the same mistakes over and over again.

I was born to be in a relationship with God. I am lonely when I'm not. And when I am disconnected, I put on others the job of taking care of my needs in a way that is impossible for them. It's at those times when I need to turn away from my anger, frustration and resentments and go inside. Get quiet. Be still. Listen.

And then get on my knees and pray the High Risk prayer.

If my life never gets any better than it is right now, am I going to be fulfilled? No.

If I want more, I must be willing to seek the changes in myself that I am desperately seeking in others.

Be the change.

Dear God.

Help me to be willing to Change!!!

Love, Susan

Isaiah 6:8 Psalm 139:23 Psalm 86:11 Jeremiah 17:10

Does Drought Bring Doubt?

As I sat quietly in church yesterday taking in all the pastor was preaching, I couldn't help but reflect on my past experiences and wonder: does drought in my life bring doubt to my faith?

The sermon was about "A Life of Worship."

Do I worship and thank God only in my times of abundance and good or do I rejoice in my droughts?

I've lived through many droughts.

Financial: those times when I just couldn't see the end of the day and believe that there was enough money to make ends meet. Again.

Emotional: those times when my heart was heavy and my soul empty. I had nothing to give to anyone. I was spent, depleted, exhausted. The fog was heavy and thick and the blackness just seemed to creep in around me and steal the light. I couldn't feel love from anyone, not even God.

Relationship: Those times when my trust level was so low that no matter how I tried, I couldn't connect to my husband, family, friends. I couldn't even connect with myself for that matter and God was so far away I almost forgot He was there.

Physical: Those times where I had no energy to do anything. My body hurt. My muscles hurt. My knees hurt. Everything hurt.

I choose the word DROUGHT today because I am exhausted from living from one crisis to another and thought there might be a better way to look at the experiences in my life so they aren't so daunting. This word seemed to fit the bill.

Last July, as my husband and I took the 5 freeway south from visiting the kids in Washington and Oregon we passed Lake Shasta. I was horrified to see how far the water had gone down and how there were small little islands beginning to poke their heads up through the water. Those islands had never been there before. Oh wait…Yes they had, but the water had covered them and now they were visible to everyone.

I wondered what would happen if the rains never came or the snow didn't fall this year. I wondered….

And the thought came to me that it really depends more on what I'm looking with, more than what I'm looking at.

Do I see the glass as half empty or half full? Do I see life and my circumstances from the point of a victim or a victor? Am I being punished by God for something I did or maybe something I didn't do? Am I always looking for the "Why me" answers to questions I don't understand?

When I looked through the trees to see the deep blue waters in Lake Shasta, where did my focus go? It went to the lack of water instead of the abundance of water. There were both, but I was looking what was missing rather than what was there.

Did I see the beautiful houseboats that lazily lingered on the edge of a cozy cove? Or the ski boats pulling water-skiers behind them, jumping the wake as they flew through the air? No. I saw the drought.

And then I got scared. I began with the "What ifs." What if there is no rain? What if the snow doesn't fall? What if the drought never stops, and what if we run out of water forever?

What happens to me when I am in a drought? What do I see?

It begins with being mindful that there is a God and He loves me, more than I can possibly know or understand. He is my provider, my counselor, my healer, my Savior. He is my everything and yet when I am living in my droughts, why do I let my mind fill with doubts?

Probably because I'm human. My default position is fear. It's what I learned growing up. Fear filled my childhood home. It lived under my parent's consciousness and, without ever saying a word, their energy flowed right over into me. Their fear became mine and permeated my cells. It became part of my DNA and has lived inside of me for a long time.

That's why when I don't stop to breathe, pray or even think, I am moved immediately into the fear of the unknown.

But when I can sit for a few minutes, be still and go quiet, I can hear the voice of God begin to whisper reminders that He is here. He is bigger than all my fears. He is bigger than all my circumstances. He is bigger than every drought.

When I am being sucked into yet another form of drought, I now make a choice to be mindful. I take time to sit, breathe and let my heart start soaking in the love of God that is always there waiting for me. I open up and accept the reassurance and peace He has for me. I listen. I praise Him. I write in my gratitude journal all the blessings I am surrounded with.

What does God reveal to me when the droughts come? Is there a little island of sanity living below my faith waters that I have never seen before? Are there other ways to look at my situations that could create a stronger reliance on God? Could the message possibly be to just relax and stop trying so hard to understand something that is impossible to figure out and turn to the faith I have inside me and trust that God has gone before me and planned my entire life out in love?

It all seems so complicated and yet so simple.

God dwells in Me and You. He lives there because He loves us and desires each of us to know Him and trust him. To live a life of worship through gratitude and thankfulness.

So the question I leave with you that was left with me yesterday is this….If I am given God's mercy every day, is what I am doing and thinking right now….giving Him glory?

Jeremiah 17:7-8 Joel 2:12 Deuteronomy 11:13-14 Leviticus 26:3-4

I Am Not a Ph.D.

I'm not a PH.D. I don't have a Master's degree in psychology. I'm not a doctor or a therapist. What I am is the mother of an addict-alcoholic. I am the mother of three. And what I know has come from my journey to hell and back with these incredible children. This is what I have experienced and have learned along the way.

Loving an alcoholic/addict is painful. Whether it be a father, mother, brother, husband, sister, friend or child, it is not an easy job.

We want to. We try. We give it everything we have. Our hearts break. Our dreams die. We fall down and get up again. We cry. And cry some more. We ask questions. We seek answers. We try to understand. The pain still comes and we choose to love anyway.

We mourn what we had hoped for. We let go of the dreams of the white picket fences and children going off to college. We mourn the loss of what we had been raised to believe would be our life. We argue with God. We try to control our lives and the lives of everyone around us. We hold on for dear life. We agonize. We bargain. We pray. The pain still comes and we choose to love anyway.

We beg. We plead. We offer advice. We suggest treatment. We give money. We bail them out of jail. We find them a job. We let them come home to live. We believe that it will be different. We give up. We give out. We sleep too much. We don't sleep at all. The pain still comes and we choose to love anyway.

I have had them all. The father. The brother. The grandfather and the husbands. The friends and distant family members. And my children. All three of them.

Loving an alcoholic and addict is what I have been called to do. It is my story. It is my family. It is my life. But more than all of these, this is my journey of discovering how my relationship with God would guide me to a peace and healing beyond my human understanding through the greatest storm of my life.

1Corinthians 13:4-8 Psalm 34:18 Romans 8:18 Jeremiah 29:11
2Corinthians 4:8-10

Fragile

Have you ever had one of those days, or two or even more when you felt fragile and didn't know why?

Where you felt so small you just wanted to hide under the bed so no one could find you?

In the past when I got these feelings, the voices from my past would scream in my head, "Buck up you scardy cat. Why are you afraid? Get over it. There's work to be done. "

I would then shudder inside my soul as I could feel my light drain through my feet, while I was engulfed in shame for having been so frightened.

Never would I let you know that I felt so lonely and afraid, especially since there was no reason for it.

I was embarrassed and because of that I would not let you in.

Instead I put on the familiar mask that says "Everything is fantastic. I am fine. The world is good." And I would walk through the day denying my feelings, swallowing my voice and living a lie.

Today I choose not to do that.

Today I will tell you when I feel fragile and I am in need of your love and support.

Today I will invite you into my world where I don't have it all together but wish I did.

Today I will honor the mess inside and not be afraid to share with you that I can't do life alone like I thought I could.

Today I will ask for help.

Matthew 7:7 Hebrews 4:16 Psalm 107:28-30 John 14:13-14

The Place of Gray

Where do you go when you slip into that shadowy place of gray where you don't feel loved, supported or accepted?

I can't say it's pitch black here, because I know there is light. And I understand this feeling is only a momentary and passing sensation of loneliness which is being manifested in my mind. My heart knows better, because God lives in my soul and I trust in His divine love and care.

But there are just times when I peer at the world through lenses of my thoughts which always create distortion to a certain degree. The all or nothing. It's perfect or awful. It's good or bad. It's black or white. I know that this is a lie I can fall into believing when I have lost my connection with God. It's the place of fear that I move into so easily without even knowing I'm going there.

It's the all too familiar which I truly despise, but I go there anyway and then find myself crying out for God's help when I feel lost......Again!

I can't fix a feeling nor will I judge it. A feeling isn't right or wrong. It just is. So I accept it for what it is, a feeling that will pass, and quicker if I stop fighting it. I will let it sit with me during a moment of quiet so it can wash over me and past me when it's ready.

Let's hope this feeling passes soon as I replace it with gratitude for having the ability and awareness to recognize where I am and be okay with my constant evolving journey to peace.

Psalm 147:3 Matthew 11:28 John 16:33 Isaiah 41:10

Intentional....

What does that mean exactly? Intentional.

According to the Thesarus.com dictionary it means:

adjective

1. done with intention or on purpose; intended: *an intentional insult.*
2. of or pertaining to intention or purpose.

That being said, it makes me wonder if I've ever been totally mindful and intentional with the life I've lived or even the things I do on a daily basis.

Does running through life at the speed of light from one project to the next, leaving behind a half finished mess, constitute intention?

Let's imagine this:

I sit down at my computer with every intention of starting and completing a simple project that should take no less than an hour.

1. Begin.
2. The house phone rings and I stop and think, "Should I answer this or wait? Maybe it's Joe's doctor calling to reschedule an appointment. The phone continues to ring. Okay. I'll make a quick side trip to answer it. How long can it take?
3. When I finally reach the phone, No answer. Dial tone. Oh well. Back to the my office.
4. Wait. The bed isn't made. I better stop for just a couple minutes and make the bed. I'll be quick.
5. Oops. The doorbell rings. Dash to the door. Man selling carpet cleaning. No thank you.
6. Glance in the kitchen. Dishes not done. Darn. I need to do the dishes. I'll quickly wash and leave them in the dish drainer.
7. Hand towels a mess. Did I forget to get the wash started before I sat down at my computer to do my project? I promised myself I would start a load of wash. Ready, set, go. To the washer.
8. I am exhausted and I haven't even started the project I was determined to complete over an hour ago.

Is it just me or does this sound like anyone you know?

I have been living life by the seat of my pants and in the fast lane since I was a kid. It was a pattern I developed to keep me busy and protect myself from the abusers in my home. If I was busy, I was productive, and productivity in my childhood home was good.

The lessons that appear to be coming face to face with me in my adult life, the patterns I created to serve my needs and guard myself from harm are now the same patterns that are creating havoc and drama in my life today.

So now what? How do I learn to let go of what I have always done to learn a new way of living? Yikes, that is a BIG question.

I'm not sure I have an answer.

But what I do know is that I am willing to make changes so I don't have to keep repeating my past mistakes and create an atmosphere of victimhood in my everyday life.

Here goes:

First I know there is a payoff for me in every choice I make. I know what you're thinking. There is no way you do what you do and like it.

You hate the results you're getting but really....if you hated them that much why are you still doing them? Why am I? What is the payoff?

Is it the feeling of familiar? I know this dance. I know the steps. Even though I am not getting what I want, is it better to do what I know than to stop, right in my tracks, admit I don't have a clue and ask for help?

You're killing me. Ask for help? Not on your life.

I have asked myself a gazillion times why it hurts me to ask for help? Does it hurt any more to ask than to suffer in silence in my own insanity of doing the same thing over and over and praying for different results.

I can do it myself. Just watch me. I'll show you. Ouch.

Who am I kidding?

The truth is that I cannot do life all by myself. I never could, but it was easier to try than to open myself up to disappointment and rejection if I asked and the help didn't come. What I learned and continue to learn is if I ask the wrong people for the right things they still cannot give me what they don't have. I can become aware of the right people who can offer what I need and ask them for help.

So where does that leave me now?

With unfinished tasks all over the house? A cluttered closet to match my cluttered mind? A feeling of frustration for not having completed what I set out to do because I have 24 hours to change the world and I don't have time to breathe much less be intentional?

Even as I write this, everything in me screams to get up and go get a cup of coffee. Go check on my husband outside. Go put the clothes in the dryer.

But today I am choosing to sit still and be intentional. Be right here, right now, in the moment, doing what's in front of me.

Begin.

Do the work.

Complete the task.

And take it one baby step at a time.

Right now outside, it's spring and change is coming.

The trees are sprouting new leaves. Flowers are beginning to bloom. Growth is in the air.

These plants are taking the time to allow God to water them, and shine sun down on their faces. They are trusting the process that when they are ready to grow it will happen.

And because they are trees and flowers they never get caught up in being anything other than what they are.

They never think themselves out of completing what they started. They let go and grow, with intention.

When have you ever seen a tree try to make a bed and do the laundry?

Today I will relax, be intentional, finish one thing at a time and let go of the internal angst.

Ephesians 5:15-16 Romans 12:2 2Peter 1:5-7 Proverbs 4:23

Thank You To My Children

As I sit here at my computer listening to Amy Grant's new song, "Don't try so hard," and editing chapter 14 and 15 of my book, Letting go of Shame, A mother's Journey raising Addict Children, I am reminded of how blessed I am to be these children's mother. I have heard people say, when asked, if they have been touched by the disease of addiction, they often reply, "Unfortunately, I have." I can only feel how fortunate I am to have been given the opportunity to love these incredible people.

My three children, Matt, Katie, and Shawn are my joy. You, my children, are my gifts. We have all lived through heartache and pain and have come around to love and respect.

YOU have given me the opportunity to grow as a woman, mom, wife and grandma. It is your presence in my life that has shown me God's love and reminded me that we all have a journey to walk, alone and with others.

I never understood the lessons I would learn through each of you. You have given me chances to make mistakes and come around and make amends. You have taught me that saying "I'm sorry" isn't enough. One has to back those words with action and stop making the same mistakes. Just because I gave you an apology doesn't make it right unless I stop doing what I did in the first place to hurt you or cause you pain.

You helped me to be more compassionate and forgiving of myself and others. If you hadn't suffered from the disease of addiction I would never have known that it was truly a disease that you didn't ask for or want. And when you told me you would quit using that you meant it at the time, but the disease was more powerful than your promises.

You didn't become an addict to embarrass me or your family. You didn't choose this road. You were born with the disease and I had to learn through my own pain and suffering to let you find your own way to recovery, even if that meant you never found it.

I came to an understanding that you were God's children and not mine. I was the one who gave birth to you, but the road you were meant to travel was created long before you were born.

Living my life as your mother has brought me to my knees in such pain and agony that I had nowhere else to go but to the arms of God. I sought His help and guidance in how to let you go so you could live freely and with dignity the life He ordained especially for you.

As I come to a place of reflection, the only words that come to me are "thank you." Thank you for being the incredible people you are. Thank you for being authentic and real and for being open with your pain and sorrows. Thank you for trusting me enough to be truthful with me and allowing me the same freedom with you even if it hurts.

YOU, my precious children, have changed my life.

YOU, my precious children, have given me the freedom to be the woman God created me to be by giving me the chance to learn how to let you be the people you were meant to be.

I am blessed beyond measure to stand and say that I have no shame for having addict children. I am the most fortunate woman in the world. YOU have enriched my soul and I will never be the same.

1 Thessalonians 5:18 James 1:17 John 14:1 Timothy 4:4-5

I Love an Addict/Alcoholic.... and I Am So Blessed.

The truth is, I love many alcoholic/addicts starting with my three children, I never knew how lucky I was to know and love these incredible people until just a couple of years ago.

It seems like these are truly the people to whom my heart gravitates. I was raised by one, married two and raised three.

I didn't start out my life knowing anything about rescuing, but I believe I was born with the nature to serve others. However, somewhere along the way, my idea of serving got distorted. I began to take care of others in ways that did not support them learning to take care of themselves.

I became the classic rescuer and enabler. I didn't mean to hurt others with my helpfulness, but slowly I began to see how my behavior was causing others more harm than good.

I would never have told you that I loved anyone with a drinking and drug problem because I carried so much shame around the fact that I felt responsible. Responsible for my dad's drinking and raging, responsible for my children's out of control behavior, and totally responsible for trying to make everything better all the time.

No one appointed me to take that job. I willingly stepped in because I was so uncomfortable when everything felt out of control. If I could anticipate what would happen next I could somehow step in and stop their anger, abuse or unacceptable choices that caused me such embarrassment and shame.

I became hyper vigilant with everyone and everything. I felt isolated and frantic, all day, every day. I didn't know what peace felt like and didn't know how to find it.

I lived this way for many years and although I adored these beautiful children I had lost sight of myself in the process of loving them. I grew angry and resentful when they wouldn't listen to my sound and sage advice. I was resentful when I would give them money only to find out later that they used it for something other than what I gave it to them for. I became so furious with their lies that I began to hate them and then hated myself for hating them.

What I really hated was their disease and my reaction to that disease. I got caught up in the whirlwind of promises and disappointments. I had trouble figuring out where they ended and I began.

As I tore my eyes away from those I so desperately wanted to help and turned my eyes back to me I started to see the deep emotional wounds I carried around with me each day. You wouldn't know it because I generally hid it well. I smiled and laughed and acted like all was good in my secret world of heartache.

Carrying the pain grew so heavy that I was forced to my knees in surrender. I was terrified of what I would feel like when I finally accepted I was not in control. Being in control was only an illusion anyway. I knew in my heart that I had to give it all up to my God, the God who loved me and my family more than I could humanly understand.

I had to let go of my dreams, aspiration, and agendas, not only for myself, but for my children. I could get real about what was important and where I stood when it came to my professed priorities. It was time for God to take hold of my hand and lead me down my own path of healing. It was my turn to allow God to work on my character defects and to open my eyes to the things I thought were so good and noble. I was given the opportunity to see myself as God had seen me all along. Frightened, lonely, angry and spiraling out of control.

I was ready to be guided to a better life, but it could only happen when I turned my will and life over to the care of God and got off the judgment seat I had sat myself on long ago. I judged what was best for all those I loved and made it my business to set them straight so they could live a long and productive life.

How dare I think I could know better than God what was right and good. Yikes, that revelation hurt to the core. I believed I was being loving and kind. Instead I was being controlling and manipulating. What I wanted was more for me and stopping my pain than it was for my children. The simple fact is this: if my children ever hurt long and hard enough they might fall to their knees and seek their own surrender to God.

I had to turn away and that's what caused my greatest heartache. Letting them go completely so they could fall into the arms of the God they believed in. I was scared to death they would die in their disease. I was afraid they would die. Period.

When I took on the role of mother I never understood the depth of joy and pain I could feel at almost the same moment. If I could love them so deeply, did that mean I could bear pain at the same level?

What I came to know is that no matter what...I loved my children. It doesn't matter whether they were an addict/alcoholic or what the world might call a successful business person, I can never take ownership of them, or their successes or failures, for they belong to God. They live the life God gave them, through me, as their mother. They were born when they were destined to be born and they would go home when God calls them home. I am powerless over that.

It is because of my children that I have a new understanding of unconditional love. It is because of my children that I was forced to my knees to learn to rely totally on a God I was unfamiliar with, until now. It is because of my children that I was given a chance to truly taste the sweetness of loving them right where they are with no judgment or bitterness. They are God's children and I am blessed to be on this journey with them. I am called to love them and trust God to lead them.

1Peter 5:7 Matthew 11:28-30 Psalm 121:1-2 Psalm 51:10-12

Living a Love Letter

In my experience it has always been easier to write a love letter than to live it.

Putting down those words to a new spouse that promise to love and cherish, in sickness and in health, till death do us part. Or those special words said to a parent or sibling that say, " I will support you no matter what because I love you."

Writing the words "I love you" look very different when we are being asked to be live them and not just say them.

Sitting down at my desk, looking out beyond the smudged windows into my newly planted yard I am reminded of all those sweet letters I penned to lovers long gone. Words that I was so desperate to convey that would make sure that this one would never leave me, walk away or abandon the woman I was trying so hard to become.

Clinging to these men like they were my life preservers who would keep me afloat of my strangling fears that whispered the lies of "You're not good enough. He's going to leave you. They all do."

I promised myself to do whatever it took to ensure I would never be left alone, and in the end, I was left alone anyway. Buying gifts to guarantee these men would feel enough guilt to stay even when they wanted to run.

I took hostages, captives in my emotional nightmare with locks on every door and bars on every window. There was no hope for escape for those I pledged to love for I never had a clue as to what love looked like or, for that matter, what it truly meant. All I knew was that at the core of my being there lived a deeply rooted monster called "fear of abandonment" and I would do whatever was necessary to protect myself from letting anyone leave my prison.

It was not pretty, and I was not brave.

It has taken years to untangle the weeds embedded in the garden of deception that I was planted in long ago. It has taken many days to understand what is a weed and what is a flower so I didn't just dig up everything, throw it all away and start over.

There were lessons in my flower bed of life and I chose to become willing to search for the buds yet to bloom and make room for the new and fragile growth wanting to birth forth in springtime.

The journey has not been an easy one, but I have been guided by a God who loves me and wants so much more for me than my human understanding can fathom.

As I look back now I feel such a deep sense of sadness at how my pain played out with those I so wanted to care for.

Today I have lived enough life experiences to know that love is real and that showing it is far different than I was taught when I was a child.

I know that love is the only thing that will allow me to fully accept you right where you are without judgment. Love is honoring your choices whether they include loving me in return or walking away. Love casts out all fear and makes room for trust and honesty. Love gives space to one another's ideas and opinions with no fear of being shamed or ridiculed. Love asks me to give you respect when making decisions to care for your own personal needs whether I understand or not. Love is choosing kindness over aggression, consideration over condemnation, charity over selfishness.

Love can only begin inside when I feel cherished and cared for by more than another human being. I must feel loved by God first, and then by myself before I can give openly and genuinely to you.

Love is who I want to be and how I want to live from this day forward.

Luke 6:35 Romans 12:9 Romans 13:10 1Corinthians 13:4-8 Ephesians 4:2

Suffering vs. Misery

Is there a difference between suffering and misery?

I believe there is.

Suffering is part of being human.

It can be the byproduct of an illness, accident or handicap that we never asked for but have been burdened to live with.

It can also come as the result of consequences due to my poor choices or the choices of someone else.

Coming from an abusive childhood I suffered physical, emotional and psychological abuse and although I never intended to be harmed by my parents, I was.

I was traumatized because of their behaviors. I don't believe they did what they did because they didn't love me, but because it was all they knew. No one can give what they never received. Hurt people hurt people.

So I grew up and began to re-create my own drama with my children the same way my parents did with me. And those choices caused my kids to suffer. It is a vicious cycle and will that until someone has the courage to find a new way and create a different and healthier path.

Suffering comes because we live out the human condition in an imperfect world.

I believe misery comes from allowing the choices I made in the past or the choices of others to continue to permeate my well-being. And when I repeat the mantra I have lived through then my misery is perpetuated by my need to be victimized regularly by the world I live in.

I was victimized. There is no denying that. It's what I was taught and it's what I know.

But somewhere along the way it becomes my responsibility to stand up against those who have harmed me either verbally or physically and scream, " Stop it. That's enough."

And there are times when I just have to tell the chatter box in my head to shut up when it wants to feed me daily lies about the unfairness of life.

It is then that I can begin the process of stepping out of my misery, deal with my moments or times of suffering and move on.

Only when I will allow myself to understand the sick cycle of abuse and crazy thinking, the acceptance of unacceptable behavior, the damage done by continued shaming and the tremendous need to stay in the pain of the familiar will I be able to find my courage, raise my voice, and stop the pain.

Being human is something I embrace, knowing that there will always be threads of heartache woven into my life journey.

But misery?

I can let that go if I make the choice to end my own victimization.

1 Peter 5:10 Romans 5:3-4 Psalm 34:19 Jeremiah 29:11

I Don't Want to Grow Up

There are days, like today, when I simply just don't want to grow up.

I'm serious. I WON'T grow up and you can't make me.

That's the conversation I am having with the 'little girl" who lives inside me. You know who I'm talking about. That little person who grabs a hold of your will and creates havoc in your life because she is not getting what she wants.

How many times have I told her to just sit down, be quiet, and let me do life the way I, the adult, need and want to do. Stay focused on the matter at hand until I'm too tired to see. Or running my day with such a fierce sense of urgency that I don't recognize that I'm hungry and haven't eaten for seven hours.

I have spent many a day ignoring that little voice that says, "I need you right now to take care of ME. I'm hungry. I'm lonely and tired and you refuse to listen. "

And that's where the trouble begins.

That's the beginning of a temper tantrum that is almost impossible to stop. The arguing that goes on inside that tells me I'm done. I quit. I am not doing this, any of this, anymore. I will NOT be responsible. I will not go to work. I will not clean my room, the house, the car or anything else that may be in front of me. I will stay in bed with the covers over my head and NEVER get up again.

Can you hear that voice? That one that makes absolutely no sense. Or does it?

Maybe all she's asking is to take some time to sit down with her and have a dialogue that matters. A conversation with myself to reason things out. How important is it to work so hard to achieve. Achieve what? Another goal that motivated me was fear of not being enough. Or a standard of excellence that looks more like perfectionism.

What exactly have I been asking of the child that lives inside this driven adult? To be perfect at any cost. To run until she can no longer stand. To be what the world is asking her to be even if it means she is not being true to herself. What am I doing and why?

I guess what I'm asking myself is how important is what I am doing right here and right now? What are my motives?

Am I wanting to be good enough in your eyes so I will feel accepted? Am I afraid of not getting what I want or losing what I have? Am I so desperate to be everyone's hero that I have totally neglected the desires of my own heart? Have I shut out God because I am too busy offering my best to the world and not offering me anything but exhaustion at the end of the day?

These are the questions I am afraid to ask because of what will I discover about myself when I learn the answers.

Today the child in me is overwhelmed with life. She's done working so hard. She's tired and wants to take a nap. She wants to eat ice cream and cookies while she watches cartoons all day long. She will do whatever it takes to get my attention. She will not give up until she gets what she wants.

And all she wants is for me to slow down long enough to hear her. Take the time to listen to what she needs.

Stop the world. I want to get off.

I get it. I know that I do my growth in a spiral motion. It just works that way for me. Peeling the onion one layer at a time. Go around once more and hear it at a different level. Hear it again and again until I really HEAR it.

Be quiet. Stop. Rest. Listen.

When I allow myself these gifts, I nurture that little girl inside who wants and needs me to cherish her and love her right where she is. When my love and time is unconditional, miracles happen.

The tantrums slowly subside as she begins to trust me. Integrating the inner child with the adult is a slow process that takes time and patience. It cannot be forced or accelerated. It must be done with intention and love. It is the miracle of growing up.

Okay. I will allow myself the space and time to grow into the beautiful woman God created me to be, and I will do it one step at a time. With a few time outs at the local rest step for maybe a tantrum, nap or simply a candy bar, we will grow because we are both worth it.

Ecclesiastes 3:7 Job 6:24 Psalm 46:10 1Chronicles 16:11 2Timothy 1:7

I Am a Painter

I had dreams about painting.

I would wake from a sound sleep to recall vivid pictures of me using paintbrushes to create scenes of color.

And I often would head into the day with a sense of awe and wonder as to why I was having these dreams and what they meant.

But I put those dreams away.

A few years later Mary Kay offered a full paint set as a prize for the Star Consultant program.

I had earned the right amount of points for this prize so the dream was reignited and I redeemed those points for the paint set.

Arriving a few weeks later, I eagerly opened it and studied all my wonderful options.

Colored pencils, watercolors, oils and chalks.

Paint brushes galore, a beautiful wooden box to hold everything and even an easel that was attached.

I was thrilled.

And then I set it down next to my husband's dresser in our back bedroom and completely forgot about it.

I put the dreams on hold, yet again.

Why?

I wondered the same thing but could not come up with an answer.

The only thing I can possibly guess was that I was too busy working, striving to reach bigger goals in my business and making a living.

I didn't have time to dabble in a hobby.

But I am learning that I don't have time to waste when it comes to using the gifts I have been richly blessed with by a loving and gracious God.

A year later my husband and I decided to take a two month driving trip across the USA to visit family and friends while seeing America close up!

We were going to make that adventure in a small Honda Civic.

I told Joseph I had to pack the paints. He looked at me with those eyes of his that often reflect his need for more information. Or the look of "Are you crazy? And how are we going to do this? Or the "Are you out of your ever loving mind?"

I was adamant and determined. I just knew that when I was sitting in a quiet and peaceful place where my soul could breathe and my mind could rest, I would paint.

And that I did, in the hills of Great Barrington, Massachusetts where we stayed on a dear friend's 35 acre farm for a month.

I breathed in the rich sunrises.

I extolled the brilliant sunsets.

I saw God's majesty painted across the skies with every breath I took and I painted.

And I breathed.

And I painted.

And oh what a joy it was.

1 Corinthians 12:4-6 James 1:17 1Peter 4:10 1Corinthians 10:31

The Washing Machine

Here I sit with that sense of a growing inner agitation beginning to take me for that familiar spin, and I wonder why I'm here again.

"Lord, seriously haven't I done enough spinning in the last couple of weeks?" I ask.

No answer. So am I safe to assume the answer is "apparently not?"

"Please don't put me back in the emotional washing machine" I plead. I'm clean enough. Right?

I don't think I will ever be clean enough. Isn't that why I'm still on my human journey? Not so much to be made perfect, for that is a human impossibility, but evidently to be cleaned and rinsed continually of my sinful nature so my relationship with God can be enriched and restored to a more intimate level.

Each time I put my clothes in the washing machine and add that little bit of soap I do it because my clothes need cleaning. Not always heavy duty cleaning but a bit of spot removing nevertheless. So into the machine they go and after 20 minutes of gentle agitation I pop them into the dryer and they come out as fresh as new. Well almost.

Isn't that simply what God is doing with me? As my soul gets soiled from living in a world where my mind takes on the grime of outside noise, my spirit absorbs pollution of thought and my heart grows weary of feeling other's pain, don't I need to be made good as new?

But I don't want to jump into that dark and cramped machine. No way.

Oh come on kid. How bad can it be? Any worse than what you're feeling right now?

In the past my restlessness was simply a reminder that I was losing control over my life. But isn't the idea of control really an illusion that I've bought into as truth?

Haven't I tried over and over to stop the twisting and turning of my mind as I've obsessed over thoughts of 'what if" and "fear?" Haven't I called out to God and begged Him to pull me away from the frozen feelings of despair that begin to swallow me up?

I don't want to live in illusions or fantasies anymore. I want to live a rich life and taste the marrow of every single experience through living with intentional mindfulness.

I silently pray, "Please God, help me find peace."

Uh. Oh. He was listening.

Grabbing a small chair, God slides it up next to His washing machine and suggests I climb up and He'll help me in.

But......

"But nothing" is His gentle response as He assures me that I won't drown, the water is not too hot and I will live through it.

"Can't I just stay out here for a few more minutes while I think of a better way?"

God's gentle smile reminds me that He is a good God and that He really wants me to be fulfilled in Him. If that means a little scrubbing behind the ears while I am being agitated, so be it.

I stop, but only for a second, because I am learning to trust my God.

And as I look down next to the washing machine I see a tiny basket holding a pair of goggles and a nose plug.

Here goes. PLOP!!!

I'm in.

And guess what? It's a big machine and there's room in here for you too.

Psalm 51:2 Leviticus 16:30 Psalm 51:10 Ezekiel 36:25

The "What Ifs"

What if my child or my husband drinks again? And what if they don't?

What if they get drunk, drive, get in an accident and kill themselves or maybe even others? And what if that never happens?

As a Mary Kay sales director who doesn't want anyone to know the secret hiding in my home, what if I don't make my production, or earn my car or lose the car I have? And what if I don't?

What if everything falls apart? And what if that's not the case?

What if I or someone I love gets sick and dies? And what if doesn't happen.

THEN WHAT?????

What if everything we are so afraid of never happens? What will we have accomplished with all the worry and energy we gave away to our fears?

NOTHING!!!

We will have only wasted the NOW we have for the future we don't have.

The only time I go into the "What ifs" is when I am so busy in my head creating scenarios that scare the life right out of me that I have nothing left to give the life I have right NOW!

STOP IT!!! STOP IT!!! STOP.... scaring yourself on purpose.

I know it's not easy to stay in the moment and trust that all is well. It's hard to be a human being especially when we are so consumed with controlling our lives and the outcomes of those lives.

We are not in control. Never have been. Never will be.

That's the plain and simple truth.

When I go into my "thinking mode" I paint pictures of the things that frighten me and then desperately try to figure out a way to stop them from happening. I go into that place because it is so familiar to me and it is easier to think than it is to feel. It is a safe space for me even though I am constantly scared when I am there. But safe means familiar and I know what to expect.

Today I know that the longest journey I will ever take is the one between my head and my heart. God lives quietly and peacefully in my heart, and my fear lives in my head. I know that, and yet I am continually led into that place of fear when things in my life are not making sense. I NEED for things to make sense.

Or do I?

I only spend time trying to make sense out of nonsense when I am far away from God, and I am having difficulty finding my way home.

I know fear. It has lived with me my whole life. I never liked it, but it was there. And I ran from it on a daily basis. Do you know what happens when you run from something that frightens you? It becomes more aggressive and runs faster to catch you. Sometimes we escape it only to have it chase us again the next day.

But when I am brave enough to stop running and turn and face the enemy, look it in the eye and stand my ground....often it turns and goes the opposite direction. I can't escape my fears unless I am willing to get on my knees and surrender my will and my life over to the care of God. And even then they don't completely go away, but they begin to subside as I begin to trust in God's divine love for me.

Maybe it's time to get off the mental Merry-Go-Round. Maybe it's time to just STOP running. To be still, right here, right now and Listen.

Could this be the time that the Holy Spirit want to whisper, "Shhh. It's all okay. No need to feed the worry monster anymore. God loves you to the moon and back and is NEVER going to abandon you. Breathe. Rest. Let go."

Is today the day that we will make the decision to stop going to the "What If" jungle or if we do, to think of all the good things that could happen instead of the bad?

It really is up to us. It doesn't matter where we came from or what we believed as truth from the past. Today we are learning that God has gone onto tomorrow and planned it all out in love.

Isaiah 41:10 Philippians 4:6-7 John 14:27 2Timothy 1:7

Shall We Dig?

Recently Joe and I let go of our gardener because he was no longer doing what he had committed to do. After sharing with him our concerns, we, continued to give him more chances to step up to the plate, but he could never quite reach it, and his work continued to come up short.

So first Joe and I discussed why we kept giving him opportunities to fix the problems when he was clearly showing us who he was and what he was capable of. Every time we gave him a second chance and he missed the mark, we were disappointed and frustrated.

But who were we really frustrated with? The gardener who had persistently tried to point out that he couldn't do the job or us for having given 100% to desperately try to change him? Good question.

After choosing to set aside our resentments and seeing that we had control over our own decisions, we decided this relationship would never work, not because he was bad at what he did but because we needed and wanted more.

Then the question became who should we hire to get out there and dig?

Our solution: We will. We hired a new "blow and go" guy to cut the grass, and Joe and I became the landscape experts. Right!!! At least we became willing to discover what the dirt might have to offer us.

I was raised by a mom who didn't like to get her hands dirty so she taught me that little girls don't play in the mud and certainly don't get dirt under their fingernails. I was quite happy letting someone else do the planting and pruning, and I would benefit from the colorful gardens once the handiwork was completed. And that's the way I felt about housework as well. Why get your hands greasy and break your back bending over a yucky toilet when you can pay someone else to do it.

So.....back to the garden.

Joe and I decided that we would go out in the back yard and together, on Sundays after I got home from church, we would begin the process of creating a masterpiece garden that we would come to love and enjoy.

Lesson #1- Nothing happens overnight no matter how fast I want it done. Growing plants requires prep work. Cleaning the flower beds, raking the leaves, turning the dirt. That means excavating! But I want instant pretty.

I would have given my whole savings account to someone, anyone who would do the emotional excavating that my soul needs? Someone to do the hard stuff for me so I don't have to hurt. But no one can do that part of my growth. I learned that the whole idea of clearing out the deeply rooted weeds in my soul is a job that God has to do, and I must be willing to show up when He is digging.

Lesson #2- Creating a masterpiece takes patience. What? Be patient? Isn't there a shortcut to beauty? Not when the job is an inside job. Rush the process, kill the plants. And then do it again. Doing the same thing and expecting different results is the definition of insanity. So how many times did I do the same ritual and then pray for results that were completely different? Over and over again until I stopped, and decided to quietly listen to other possibilities.

Lesson #3- Be clear on your expectations. If I plant yellow flowers it wouldn't do me any good to shout at God when I didn't get orange flowers blooming from my garden. What did I plant anyway? Was I even looking at the seeds I bought or did I just haphazardly pick up the cheapest seeds at the dollar store? Oh you mean there is a place I can go to ask questions and get the right plants and flowers? There is a perfect plant to go in a perfect spot? Hm....now that's a concept. What seeds have I been planting in my heart and are they the right ones to bring about the growth that I am hoping for? Did I take the time to look at the seeds I chose and take the ones marked gratitude, acceptance, faith and love, or did I grab the seeds labeled resentment, anger, greed and envy. OOPS!!!

Lesson #4- If you are going to invest time and energy then tend the garden after it's planted. You mean I can't plant it, walk away and think it will take care of itself? Nope!!! Only if you plant fake flowers. But is that really what you want?

Time. Time. Time. Quiet time. Special time. Scheduled time. Intentional time. That's what it takes to not only plant it, but tend to it. I have to decide to spend time with my garden if I want it to be beautiful. Pulling weeds, digging out rocks, raking the leaves, and pruning. Do I need to spend that much time with God so He can do the same with me? I know that I MUST be willing to allow God to prune from me the branches that bear no fruit, but letting Him cut them off, break off the negative spirit that crops up like a weed around my soul? I think that's going to hurt. Who am I kidding? I KNOW that's going to hurt. But am I worth it?

Lesson #5- The one who does the work reaps the benefits. When the gardener works with the earth, seeds, water and sun the plants flourish, and he looks at what he took the time to nurture and he smiles. He sees the breathtaking wonder he created with his own hands, and his spirit lives in the exquisite beauty of his masterpiece.

That's how God must feel when He chooses to create His masterpiece in me. He wants to take His time and tend to me, nurture me and water me with His unending love and joy. However, it comes with a cost. Am I prepared to be pruned of the things that harm myself and others? Am I willing to sit still through the process so that beauty can be brought forth through my presence? Can I endure God's deliberate excavation so He can shine His light though me?

As I quietly gaze at the gardens in the backyard and observe the slow beauty that unfolds with the passing of each day, I can only nod in agreement when God asks, "Shall we dig?"

Hosea 10:12 James 3:18 Galatians 6:9 2Corinthians 9:6-8

Financial Security vs. Financial Serenity

I am not sure I will ever reach the place where I feel financially secure in a world that revolves around money and power.

Besides, how much is enough?

When will I feel safe enough to let go and trust God? After I have won the Lotto or inherited a boatload of money from a dying relative?

Will I ever be comfortable spending what I have socked away for a rainy day when it is really needed?

I have spent much of my life living with a mentality of "not enough," not because I want to accept that as truth, but because that idea was so ingrained into my psyche from childhood that the belief just lives there.

So now my struggle is to let go of the fear that creeps in whenever I take time away to visit family and friends. To stop the cycle of quietly counting every dime I spend as I nourish the love relationships I have through sharing time together. To cease the mental chatter that feeds my mind with the fear of losing everything I have worked so hard for if I take too much time to play and have fun.

Why have I spent my entire life working if all I do is worry about using the earned money to enjoy the life I have now?

Thus the idea of financial serenity.

I don't need a lot of money to be financially serene if I have a trust relationship with God.

If each day I can focus on the NOW, I will be more prepared to live life one day at a time. I will start believing that my needs will be met and then slowly and cautiously I can begin taking baby steps towards letting go of my need to voraciously work to put more money in the bank for tomorrow.

When I operate from the place of lack, I am at risk of losing relationships in the moment. When I refuse to let go of my control by offering up to God my fears about the future, I live in scarcity and sorrow.

There may be no tomorrow. I get that, and yet I find myself trying to stock pile for a day, a week or a month from now, almost like I am demanding that God give more than I need so I can breathe more easily.

Will I ever live with God's ease, balance and grace as I learn to respectfully use what God has blessed me with? Can I give myself the freedom to enjoy the company of those I love over a shared meal, or a weekend away from the phones and hectic schedule of everyday life, or simply paying for coffee for a stranger in need?

I am talking about trusting the fact that I have been cared for my entire life. I have never gone without a place to lay my head at night after a difficult day, or a meal to fill my belly when the hunger monster starts to roar or a job that allows me the space and freedom to do what I love.

Has there always been everything I need right when I needed it? Absolutely.

Has it been enough? As a woman who chooses to believe in God I can say yes, but as a human who gets pulled into a world of "you must have more, and be better and bigger to survive," that answer is no.

So now what? Who do I want to be and how do I want to live?

Today I will seek the will of God in everything I do. I will quiet my mind and listen for the small voice that gives me direction. I will be grateful to have the ability to do the next indicated step even if all that means is doing the dishes. I will take the action necessary to build a relationship with God based on "thank you" instead of "give me."

And most importantly I will surrender my bank account to the God who has always managed to make sure there is something there for a rainy day.

Matthew 6:11 Philippians 4:19 Psalm 81:10 Hebrews 13:5

Forced-Fed GOD

I remember being taught early about God and it wasn't a lesson taught with unconditional love.

That god, from the time I was a toddler, was a god who kept score. A god who hid behind closed doors spying on me to see everything I did wrong. And then couldn't wait to get a hold of me and make me pay for all my digressions.

I understand today that my concept of god was wrapped tightly around my first experiences with my human father, an angry and punishing dad who lashed out and used violence to control and manipulate us. It was what he learned growing up and passed it down right onto us. I don't blame him anymore, but I did for a long time.

Church was not a house of worship for my family. Well at least it wasn't what I was being shown by my parent's behavior. Church was where we went each Sunday, all dressed up clean and pretty to make an appearance on what a good family looked like.

We all walked in together with smiles on our faces, but if any one of us kids began to get restless, we were quietly marched outside, given a beating, told to smother our cries and suck down our tears as we silently strolled back in like nothing happened.

Having lived through these experiences it was extremely difficult for me to accept that God was a kind and loving father who only wanted to love and protect me. Not on your life was I ever going to give in to the god I was taught about growing up.

It was like being fed spinach at the dining room table and as I gagged and almost threw up all over my dinner plate, my mom would say "Just take one more bite. You'll like it."

Was it that hard to see that I clearly didn't like it? And I wouldn't like it the next time or the next. Force feeding me something I didn't like was not going to make me enjoy it later.

I do recall after I had my first son, my husband and I were fed a beautiful steak dinner, while still in the hospital, to celebrate the birth of our child. I love steak but there on the plate was a pile of spinach. "Spinach," I thought to myself. It has been a long time since I tried this stuff. Maybe now I could taste it and like it. Nope. Took a bite. Gagged again. And then proceeded to vomit.

I never wanted to be forced to eat or believe anything that turned my stomach, whether it be food or a spiritual concept. I knew in my soul, from the beginning, what felt true and what was a lie. I had to find my own path as I grew up.

I turned away from organized religion so I could clear my head and my heart. It's not that I stopped believing in God, I just needed to separate myself from the god of my childhood so I could clearly choose the God of my adulthood.

I had to take ownership of my life and my faith.

I remember how desperate I was for my addict children to like, enjoy and participate in school. I prodded them to get good grades so they could go to college and succeed.

Who was I kidding? They hated school and made it clear to me that they would make their own choices and live with their own consequences. I pleaded with them to listen to my sage counsel and continually informed them that they would regret their decisions later in life if they didn't follow my instruction.

I force fed them the idea that I knew what was best for them. They not only turned away from me later on, but from the God I had taught them about. The same God I had turned away from at the same age.

Now what?

It took a lot of time and many painful and disastrous events to turn me around and point me in a direction where I even wanted to find God again. I was forced to my knees when it came to my children. I was exhausted from raising addict kids and finally, when I had no place to go and my heart was in daily turmoil, I went looking for the God I had so conveniently locked away. I slowly began my journey back.

I was defeated, depleted and despondent.

And that was my starting point of reaching out and up to someone who had been there all along.

I wasn't sure how to go about trusting this God, but deep down inside, buried under all the remnants of the lies I had been fed, I knew there was a power greater than me and I was hungry to find my God.

Proverbs 8:17 Deuteronomy 4:29 Jeremiah 29:13 Hebrews 11:6

Someone Just Pushed the Shame Button

How often do we, without knowing, either say something that triggers another's shame or have someone do the same thing to us?

Do you even know what your shame trigger is and how do you know when it has been touched and detonated?

It has taken me a lifetime to even begin understanding shame and knowing that I've carried it at the deepest level of my soul for as long as I've been alive.

Shame has been talked about as the concept of not making a mistake but rather, BEING the mistake.

As I pondered this idea I thought, "Oh that's definitely not me. I have never felt like I was a mistake. So no problem for me. Shame is not on my radar."

It was never in my thought process because it lived secretly below my level of comprehension or understanding. It was a quiet ache that lurked in my soul and was covered up with my hunger for sugar, approval from others or my quest for perfection.

It was a monster looking to be fed, and without realizing it, I fed it every day.

I questioned myself regularly, but I thought that was a good habit because it meant I was being diligent about being on task and thorough.

I compared my insides with your outsides, but thought that was just my way of wanting to become a better person.

I struggled daily to do everything right because I was taught if I do anything at all I must do it "right" in the first place. "Right" is open for interpretation, by the way. Whose definition of right was I trying so hard to conform to?

I walked on egg shells around angry people because I thought that was the way of being a peacemaker and keeping everything in balance.

And I never looked, REALLY looked at my family of origin because I thought my family was perfect and I loved them. Why look for anything derogatory when there is so much good to see?

What I discovered was my behavior was all triggered by my secret shame.

I questioned myself daily about my choices because I lacked confidence in all areas of my life. I may have looked like I had things in control, but if you opened up my soul you would have seen terror and fear carved over every inch.

I compared myself to you because, in my mind, I was never enough. You were always so far ahead of me, earning more prizes, getting more recognition and achieving more success. And I was always sucking your wind. It was a dreadful place to be, but I was familiar with that spot of always trying to measure up.

And what if I made a mistake? What if I told you I was going to do something and I forgot? What would I tell you when you asked for the results? I would most likely make something up and lie to you about how I had tried when I had made no effort at all. What if I did do what you had asked and failed miserably? How could I be open and honest and truthful when I carried the shame of being defective? There must be something wrong with me if I couldn't be successful at what I'd been instructed to do.

I would simply tuck my shame between my heart and soul and run away.

Being a peacemaker in my family and the family hero was a shield I wore with pride. I would make it all better. I would rush to your aid and fix your pain. I would smooth over anyone's anger and keep everyone safe. That was simply because I had swallowed my voice for so long that there were no words left to scream out my rage for having been harmed and abused by others. The thought of speaking my truth horrified me and I suffered in silence as I continued to stifle my wrath. Shame took away my ability to speak up and defend myself.

And lastly I refused to look deeper into my family and the actions taken by me and against me as a child because then I would have to stand face to face with a realty that not only caused me distress then, but continued to seep into my adult life and wreak havoc today.

I am the product of my childhood. The beliefs I was taught, the lies I was told, the dysfunctional system I believed was honorable and true.

Until today....

Today my journey has opened my eyes to truths I never thought I would embrace much less understand.

The shame I have carried was never mine in the first place. It belonged to my parents, and their parents and those who raised them. It was passed down from generation to generation and to my sadness and sorrow I passed it on to my children.

But we don't have to accept anyone else's truth as our own. We can begin the process to think for ourselves. We can start opening our mouths and speak up. We can come together and recognize that we all deserve to live a life of freedom from judgment, not only by others but, more importantly, freedom from our own personal judgments. It is okay to stop believing our own lies.

The time has come to breathe in courage and let go of the bitterness, resentment and anger that has distorted our life and how we see our world.

We were born enough. We are still enough, and no matter what happens along the way we will always be ENOUGH!

Isaiah 54:4 Psalm 26:3 Psalm 119:78 Psalm 25:2

The Gift

My greatest joy and greatest sorrow has been wrapped up in one beautiful gift.

The gift of my children.

These incredible people have, on numerous occasions, brought me to my knees at the foot of my Lord.

I have cried out in my sadness for their pain.

Watched them fall from grace because of alcohol and drugs.

Listened to their cries of desperation and felt powerless to help.

Laid in bed at night while my tears fell until my eyelids were too heavy to hold up.

I have learned the meaning of surrender.

And I have come to an understanding that I serve a God who loves me and my children beyond any human ability to fully comprehend the depth of that love.

I have watched each of them struggle to find their way, pulling themselves up from the gutters of their past and make new choices.

I have rejoiced in their successes and been blessed to see them grow into incredible adults.

I have loved them and cherished them every step of the way.

Today I know I cannot take responsibility for their failures any more than I can take credit for their successes.

I have been chosen the do the best I can to be an example of love and kindness while staying out of God's way as He leads them each down their own path of life.

I have learned a new way to live and love.

And all because I have been called to be a.....MOTHER!

Isaiah 49:15 Psalm 139:13 Proverbs 31:25-31 Proverbs 23:25

I Am a Wife

I have carried the title of wife three times. This is not something I am proud of, but today it is a reality I am no longer ashamed of.

My first husband was an alcoholic who left when our children were two, three and seven. He came home from a tour overseas and after a year, he decided he just couldn't stay. He left and shortly thereafter he married again and moved out of state.

I married my second husband when he was five years clean and sober. With ten years under our belt he went back out and started using drugs again. After my children found his drug paraphernalia I turned him into the police. He was arrested for attempted manufacturing of methamphetamines. I filed for divorce while he was in jail.

Pretty simple and yet, very sad.

Today is so different.

The marriage I have now is a union of two people who are dedicated to one another during the hardest and best of times. Our personal growth and relationships with God are different as

I am a Christian and he is a Jew. Joseph and I love one another and are committed to working through every sorrow and every joy together as we navigate the challenges of our personal lives and the life we live as a couple.

What I have learned along the way is that just because I have a wedding ring on my finger and a certificate in the safe deposit box, that doesn't mean I am in a healthy marriage.

I have taken responsibility for the part I played in the failure of my first two marriages, and suffered through a lot of guilt. I know today that I cannot control another human being's choices. I can do only my part. Trying to convince another person to stay in a relationship and work things out only creates drama and heartache. It has to be a free choice made by both.

Yes I made my mistakes. I wasn't the best communicator. I wasn't always supportive. I got angry and said harsh words. And I never nurtured the relationships. Living a healthy marriage wasn't modeled for me, but I did do the best I could with the tools I had. And so did the men I was married to. It takes two to either mend or destroy a marriage, and we each played our own roles in the demise of these relationships.

We just weren't equipped to do better, so the unions ended and left collateral damage in their wakes.

After 21 years in 12 step programs, I now have tools that help me learn what role I play in my relationships with all those I love.

I take ownership of what is mine, and let go of what belongs to someone else. I make every effort to give more than I take, and practice gratitude daily. I make a commitment each day to look at the man I love through the eyes of love and let the little things fall away.

Marriage means more to me today than it ever did. It means work, time, focus and energy.

Because something worth loving, truly loving, is worth cherishing, honoring and saving.

Romans12:9 1Corinthians 13:4-8 1Corinthians 13:13 Ephesians 4:2

We All Have a Story

We are all unique. There will be no one other than you that will live the life you have been given. It's yours and was designed just for you.

And it's time that we each tell our story in our own words to the world.

Have you ever wondered what it would be like to let the walls down from around your heart, step out from behind your fears and get real?

Have you ever thought about what it would feel like to really tell your truth without fear of judgment or ridicule? To use your voice for something you were passionate about not caring what anyone thought or said?

Are you tired of living your life for others instead of living your own life?

I know how that feels. I have known for a long time but I never took the risk to change. I have waited for others to make a way for me. But no more. Not now. It's time.

I hunger for your truth, your honesty, your authenticity.

I want to hear your voice. See your eyes. Watch you smile. I want to know you.

And until we all grab a hold of our courage and stop pretending that we have it all together no one will ever know who we are, what we love and the principles we stand for.

We are RAW- real, authentic women.

I invite you to join us as we come together as women of all ages and backgrounds to create change in our world.

It's time to stop living in the shadows of our secrets for we are not defined by our mistakes. We are changed through them and if no one knows of our honest experience how can any of us grow in the light of our individual uniqueness and power.

It is in our weakness that we grow strong.

Come take a journey with us and open some doors you may have never even known were closed.

Come alongside your sisters and open up your secrets and sorrows so we can cherish one another. Begin to breathe deeply the truth of who we are and how we matter to one another.

Let go of your shame. Stand up tall, and let you voice be heard.

We want to hear you.

1Timothy 4:4 Romans 12: 6-7 2Corinthians 5:17 Jeremiah 1:5

High School Reunion

Marywood. Final school reunion. Was I going?

I didn't know anything about it until a former classmate Facebooked me and asked if I was planning on attending. It was Thursday and the reunion was Saturday.

Should I go?

Should I not?

I put the thought away until the morning of the event, and as I sat with God during my quiet time, these were my thoughts.

If I go what should I wear. So here I was at 60 years old trying to feel like I'm good enough all over again.

Why does it matter?

Who did I ever feel close enough to back then to care enough today.

I never felt like I fit in.

I was not a jock nor one of the smart girls. I had few friends. Mostly I was a loner, because it was safer that way.

With only one best friend who wasn't going to be there the question became "do I really need to see the school one last time to move on with my life today?"

Should I go to say goodbye?

To remember?

To forgive?

To let go?

I didn't want to go to try to measure up to anyone for anything. To try to connect with people I never had a connection with in the first place.

I surely didn't want to fall into the trap of thinking that this time it would be different. This time would I be embraced by those I used to watch from a distance and wonder what it would be like to be them? Or would I be remembered and people would be glad to see me because they had missed me all these years?

If I decided to go it would be because this private girl's catholic high school up on a hill was my school too.

It really didn't much matter today if I played on the basketball team, or was part of the debate team (I was a part of neither) or the head cheerleader.

What mattered was this school held four years of my life and memories to go along with it.

There were times when we would sit out on the patio outside the cafeteria overlooking the 55 freeway with our uniform skirts pulled up, our knee socks pushed down and our shirts tucked into our bras, lathered up with baby oil trying to get a quick tan during study hall.

And there was the time Jerri and I ditched Mass, snuck away from the crowd and took her little white car down the hill for breakfast at Denny's!

And then there was the big one when Carol, Jerri and I walked home (20 miles) on our last day of senior year to Costa Mesa from the top of the hill just so we could say we did it.

Surely I could not to forget that fall I took on the wet concrete going to the car that drove me home every day. I got my bright, lime green petty pants under my skirt soaking wet so we decided it would be a great idea to fly that undergarment from the antenna on Mary Ann's mom's old Chevy.

There were father daughter dinner dances where my dad tried to teach me how to fox trot. There were times we both agreed to bring my best friend along because she had no dad, and we wanted her to feel loved, cherished and included.

If I went today, it was because it was vital to bring back to my consciousness some of those memories that helped create the woman I am today.

But would I have the strength to stand tall with courage, and be the successful woman I am today?

Did I go?

I did.

Was it different than all those years ago?

Not really.

In some ways it was more painful, because I got to see that not a lot had changed.

Not the school, not the women.

Yes we had aged, some more gracefully than others.

One girl who wasn't my friend 45 years ago stood next to me, looked at my name tag, spoke my name, scrunched up her nose and walked away.

So there it was.

Again.

As I thought of hanging my head like I would have so many years ago, I realized I had a choice today.

I could give my power away, or I could hold my head up, take ownership of who I am, and walk away proudly knowing that I had not done that to her. Not now. Not ever.

The thoughts kept tumbling through my spirit.

Who were we really? Back then we all hungered to find our tribe, our people, our place to fit in.

Did I even have people?

I had wondered how I would make it through those four years?

Who would carry me through those moments when I was too afraid to let anyone know that the secrets in my home were killing my spirit?

Were we the same scared and lonely, insecure and fearful women putting on a front so somehow we could keep our family secrets at bay? Was our shame hidden? Was darkness pushed down inside of us to the point of using drugs to squash our ever present pain of "not enough's?"

I don't know from looking at those women today if anything had changed other than their bodies, face and hair color.

But what I do know is that it was a beautiful day to stand up and be the messy, unfinished masterpiece that I am.

I was not a part of the clique then and I wasn't going back to be part of the clique now.

But I still had every right to show up, to be there, to see where four years of my life were spent.

I still had the right to be part of those memories for they belonged to me.

I would go to remember.

To embrace the woman I am today for having had these years to shape me.

To give myself the gift of putting more puzzle pieces in place as I continue to discover who I was, who I am and who I strive to be.

I would go because today it doesn't matter who I see before me. What matters is who I see within me.

A child of God born to shine.

Luke 6:26 2John 15:18-20 1Peter 3:14 Proverbs 13:20-21

What I Didn't Want You to Know

For more than half my life I have been self employed in a business that focuses on beauty. The idea being that when a woman feels beautiful on the outside, her inner being starts to change.

There have been more times than I can remember when I sat across the table from a woman who shared her heart with me, stories of how she felt ugly, unwanted and often times, very alone. And as we spent time together, I poured my energy and attention into her, and watched as she was transformed right before our eyes. Her spirit lifted. She smiled. Her eyes lit up and her heart softened.

It's why I came into this business. Not to sell products to women who didn't have a need, but to share a company and a line of skin care that really makes a difference. Was it just the products that provided a way to make those changes? No it was the relationship we built as friends along with the Mary Kay products, that brought about an enriching and lasting experience for us both.

Friends that have lasted a lifetime are one of the many gifts this business has afforded me.

So I have dedicated myself to pampering, encouraging and enriching the lives of others through sharing the Mary Kay experience.

It is beautiful and magical all at the same time.

But what you didn't know was the pain that silently lurked under my smile and the shame that was hidden as well.

I had secrets.

Secrets that I just couldn't bear to share with anyone.

Secrets that kept me from being authentic and real for fear if you really knew my story you would abandon me and never do business with me again.

One of my secrets was during my journey as a Mary Kay Sales Director, I had become a divorced woman whose husband had left for another woman.

It's not that I was embarrassed about being divorced. I knew many women who had gone through what I was going through. It was more the idea that my first husband walked out and moved on to another relationship, leaving me with the responsibility of raising our children.

What was wrong with me that I couldn't manage to keep my marriage intact? What could I have done differently to ensure my husband would stay?

How could I show up on your door step with a smile on my face and come in to give you my complete and total attention when I felt so alone and empty?

I was ashamed and didn't want you to know.

My second marriage ended after my children brought me drug paraphernalia and asked me to do something about it. I knew there were serious ramifications that could result if I did nothing, so I went to the police and I turned my husband in.

Seriously what would you have thought if you knew my husband was selling drugs from our garage back door and I was selling you mascara from the front door at the same time?

I didn't even want to imagine how that information would affect our relationship. I couldn't afford to let that secret out for fear that my business would be destroyed and I wouldn't have the money to raise my children.

I was lucky that none of this information was ever published in the local newspaper's headlines or that my kids were taken from me and given to my ex husband.

I could barley breathe as I served this man divorce papers while he was in jail.

Even writing about this now brings pain to my soul as I relive what could have happened to my family if I sat on the sidelines in denial and pretended, yet again, that nothing was wrong.

I knew something felt suspicious, but I didn't want to know what that something was.

Until I couldn't look away any longer.

But the biggest secret I was desperate to keep was that I had three beautiful children who were struggling with the disease of addiction.

My oldest was out of the house by the time I knew he was involved with Cocaine. My daughter and youngest son were still at home, one struggling with meth and the other with alcohol and marijuana.

Twice divorced, all I could hear were those voices in my head screaming "loser" and shame continuing to eat me alive as I left my house with my beauty case going out into the world to bring about change for good.

I cried at night when I thought about how helpless I felt watching my children fall into the dark hole of drug addiction.

How could I stand before anyone and tell them that I was in a "Pretty" business when my home life was so messy?

What would you think of me if you knew one of my children was in jail for using a stolen credit card and I let him sit there refusing to pay his bail?

Or that I was called to the high school office because my son was caught trying to sell drugs on campus?

The sorrow I carried with me each day was monstrous and I dreaded the possibility that if you found out the truth you would completely reject me.

How could I expect to be successful with so much drama surrounding me day after day?

Please allow me to share with you what I learned as I continued to seek God and allow Him to grow my strength and courage.

1. I came to the understanding that my children suffered from a disease. Not everyone believes that addiction is a disease. Some think that if I was a stricter parent, had a deeper belief in God, or if I had not gotten a divorce, my kids would not have chosen this road.

My children never chose this road. They were born with the disease of addiction. They never looked up at me when they were little and said, "Mommy, when I grow up I want to be an addict."

2. It was never my fault that they were afflicted with this disease. I didn't cause it. I couldn't cure it and I most certainly couldn't control it.
3. No matter what I did my heart still hurt. And what I was trying to do when I "helped them" was really making every effort to ease my own deep sorrow and sadness.

I thought I was helping when I gave them money, tried to get them a job, did their homework so they wouldn't fail or paid their debts. What I learned was if they were hurting enough, they would be forced to seek their own answers. I could never do enough to spare them from their own consequences.

4. I didn't have to be a victim to their choices and what I had to do was find my own answers. I joined a 12 step program with others who were struggling the same way I was and let them help me out of the darkness.
5. I developed an even stronger relationship with God, getting on my knees and surrendering my children, my life and my lack of understanding to God.
6. And I chose to speak about what caused me to be so quiet and lose my voice.

I shared my story. I opened up. I told my truth and shined light onto my shame and embarrassment.

When I became brave, I found there were others who were walking that road with me and I wasn't ALONE.

I discovered in my willingness to be vulnerable, real and authentic, you encouraged me, supported me and loved me.

You never intended to stop doing business with me just because I had challenges in my life that caused a mother's heart to hurt.

You came along side me and shared my pain.

And in the end, we all came to know and love one another even more.

If you feel you need to hide the fact that you or someone you love suffers from alcoholism or drug addiction, you don't have to swallow your voice or hide your shame.

Our secrets keep us bound, but our truth opens us up for healing.

You are not alone. There are others who are on this journey too and you don't have to be lonely in your heartache.

We stand together.

Ecclesiastes 4:9 Ephesians 4:32 Galatians 6:2 1Thessalonians 5:11

When the Giver Can't Give

Throughout my life I have always considered myself a giver. I love the feeling I get when given the opportunity to help another human being, whether it be a $1 to a homeless man standing on the freeway ramp, an Angel Blanket for someone in crisis, a listening ear for a friend who needs to talk, or a neighbor who needs a meal.

Giving is just in my nature.

It's what I do.

It's who I am.

I have lived my life wanting to make a difference in my world though the act of sharing and kindness.

Recently I had a chance to talk with a special like-hearted friend about financial giving. We both have loved the idea of offering financial aid to families in trouble. Buying dinner for an entire group of teenagers. Doing a whole Christmas for a widow and her children.

But situations change and the extra cash is not available like it used to be.

So now what? What does it mean?

I don't have the freedom to do the things I have done in the past. And I miss the chances I used to have to "save the day."

As we rode along talking about the ins and outs of giving and receiving we wondered why life had taken such a turn.

Then it dawned on me like a light bulb going on in a dark closet. Giving isn't just about money.

In fact, it is so much more.

Giving of our time.

Giving of our friendship.

Giving from our heart.

These are the gifts that money can't buy.

These are the gifts of the heart that can only come from a heart that knows how to love.

Sometimes God has to step in and hold us back so He can move someone else in to the place of giver.

The example that came to mind was when my youngest brother needed a kidney transplant. All four of his siblings stepped forward to be tested and were willing to be the donor if we were a match.

Three of the four of us tested first, myself and my two brothers.

I ended up being a perfect match.

Our family was thrilled and, as the oldest child, I felt especially honored as I had left home when my brother was only five and I was looking forward to building a more intimate relationship through this process.

My younger brothers and my only sister breathed a huge sigh of relief that I was the "CHOSEN" one and later shared with me that they weren't really worried about having to step up because "Susan will do it. That's what she does."

After further testing, UCLA decided that although I had a six out of six antigen match I was not the best candidate. Because of my controlled high blood pressure, the doctors determined that they, in good conscious, couldn't risk taking a kidney from someone who might later suffer challenges with kidney function due to hypertension.

I was devastated. I was sad. I was even angry.

How dare I not be able to give this to my brother? Don't you get it God?

I'm the giver. This is what I do. This is who I am.

I cried. My brother cried.

The three remaining siblings were dumbfounded.

If Susan can't do it, who's going to do it? No one knew what to do, and if felt like our world had suddenly turned upside down. We thought we had it all figured out.

Now what happens?

After much discussion and further testing our number two brother stepped in and gave his kidney.

What I learned through this was that the giver who always rushes in to be the hero often denies another the rewards of being the gift bearer.

My brother gave the gift of a new life to our youngest brother.

The giver was enriched in ways that words can't describe.

And life for these men will never be the same.

I learned that being the giver all the time takes blessings away from those who couldn't give because I took over.

Giving brings joy.

Giving brings renewal of the heart.

Giving brings about change.

I love to give.

And in my not giving I realized that I am, in fact, still giving another human being an experience to embrace the rewards of their own generosity.

Everyone is really a giver and receiver. We are all part of the whole woven together in a circle of ongoing eternal love.

Proverbs 11:24-25 Matthew 10:42 Galatians 6:2 Proverbs 18:16

Pain, Perception and Forgiveness

This morning during my quiet time I had a chance to reflect on pain, perception and forgiveness.

I was brought back to a time in my life when something I said was taken out of context and someone I loved was hurt.

After that person shared with me that what I said caused her pain (which took a great amount of courage to put her vulnerability out there) I got angry.

I was furious with them because what I said was not mean, never meant to be taken as mean spirited, and was totally exaggerated on their part.

Their perception was clearly off by a mile.

But what I realized later was that my anger was a byproduct of embarrassment. I felt some shame for having harmed the spirit of someone I cared about whether it was intentional on my part or not.

Perception is reality, but it doesn't mean it's true.

I perceived that what I spoke was harmless.

Their perception was different, and they were offended.

I stopped.... In my emotional tracks and listened to my heart.

What now?

I harmed someone I loved and the only thing I could do was ask for their forgiveness.

It didn't matter who was right or wrong.

What mattered was that I hurt another human being.

And today I know, at my core, if I ever again speak a word or flash a look that brings harm to another person's spirit, I will again ask for their forgiveness.

For it is in asking for forgiveness that relationships are restored and hearts are mended.

Ephesians 4:31-32 Matthew 6:12 Colossians 3:13 Ephesians 4:32

The Garden

Every chapter of my life is like a new garden.

Freshly planted with new ideas, dreams of how it's going to grow into the most magnificent colorful paradise I have ever seen, and promises that I will take the time to enjoy it.

Rich colors of experiences coupled with delightful hues of memories as they weave throughout the encounters chosen by me and offered by others.

As I step back and observe, I am filled with hope. The garden is fresh, clean and filled with possibilities.

And then I begin to see some weeds.

In the beginning there are only a few so I simply look away and focus on the new life recently planted.

But as time continues to move on and the fresh seeds begin to flourish, the weeds do too.

The water I give to the garden is the same water that feeds the weeds.

So do I stop giving my garden the water it needs to thrive so that I can control the growth of the weeds?

Nope.

Up until recently my pattern was to look at my little oasis, observe the weeds, dig up EVERYTHING and start over.

It seemed so much easier.

But in the long run it was so much more work than tending to the weeds as they appeared.

My first mistake was allowing my own denial to set in, looking the other way and pretending not to see them in the first place.

That simply prolonged the problem.

That's what denial does.

It makes the problem bigger while we work so hard at not seeing it.

There must be another way, and we all know it's not the easy way.

Caring for the garden takes work, determination, commitment and a vision that beyond the work, there is beauty.

Creating something beautiful and worthwhile means I have to put my heart and soul into it.

I must be mindful, willing to do the tiresome work of discovering where the flowers end and the weeds begin.

Sifting through the mess to find the gifts of growth.

Lifting up the dead leaves so I can discover the rich earth underneath.

There is nothing quick about creating and cultivating a garden that captivates the heart with its breathless beauty.

This is how God works in my life.

If I am willing to surrender my will and my life He can tend to the flowers and the weeds both.

My heart is the garden and sin is the weeds.

Only God can pull out and discard the deep roots of my sinful nature and character defects when He is ready, not just when I'm ready.

In my deepest desire to be all that He has created me to be, my heart can be cleansed and I will be made new.

For He is God.

Isaiah 58:11 Psalm 51:10 Romans 12:2 Proverbs 23:26

Perfectionism

"Momma I want to be perfect."

"Why baby? Why do you want to be perfect?"

"So I can get some friends."

"You don't have any friends?" I ask.

"Not very many."

"Why?"

"'Cause I'm just not like them. We don't have a lot of money, and you're only a waitress. Daddy is gone and our car is old. They're all pretty and I'm not."

Oh how my heart would break if my daughter thought she had to be perfect just to get friends.

How would I respond to her? What would I say if this were a conversation that I'd actually had?

I would tell her that she is perfect the way she is, and that she doesn't have to prove herself to anyone.

It doesn't matter what kind of car we drive, what house we live in, whether our daddies are here or have gone away. And certainly not the job titles we wear.

I would tell her she is deserving of love and respect no matter what.

I would tell her that she doesn't need to compromise who she is or what she values to get someone to like her or pay attention to her.

I would breathe belief I have into my precious daughter that no matter what anyone says, she is beautiful, kind, loving, special, talented in her own wonderful ways and that never, never does she have to prove her worth.

I would remind her that she is a child of God, and that she's valuable to me as her mother and to God as His daughter.

But somewhere in there I would have to stop and look at my own issues around feeling deserving of love. I would have to take a look at why I feel I have to be perfect in my world today to be considered a good businesswoman, a good wife, a good friend.

This all brings me to the recent Leadership Conference I attended in Nashville for our company. I traveled with a dear friend and we each said a prayer at the start of the new day that we would keep our eyes on the Lord, not look around, not compare and not judge.

We couldn't even walk down the hallway to the elevators before we saw other women and began to criticize the way they looked, the hair they had or the shoes they wore.

"What's wrong with us?" I asked as we continued down to the buses.

"We can't even get to the first floor before we are right in the middle of it again, and we just barley said amen."

As we walked silently out the swinging hotel doors I couldn't help but realize that I only judge others when I feel not good enough or that I don't measure up to those around me. Why do I think I need to be perfect to belong or feel loved?

Whose voices are those that rumble around in my head telling me that I'm not smart enough or pretty enough?

They are definitely not the voices of God who loves me.

These are the voices of my past. The people in my life who felt shame, and then passed those feelings on to me. My parents, my teachers, my boyfriends and girlfriends and sometimes even the neighbors.

And especially the world.

I understand our desperate need and overwhelming desire to be connected. A yearning that is so big we almost can't find the words to describe it.

To know we belong somewhere with someone.

It is part of our DNA.

But at what cost?

Do we have to die to who we are in order to be accepted by our fellows or is it just the opposite?

When we claim who we are at our core, holding true to our beliefs and sharing our voice, is it then that we are embraced by others who walk the same journey and seek the same connections?

I believe that when we can lovingly accept who we are at our best and our messiest, laugh at our mistakes and cry for our brokenness, reach out to others and break our cycles of shame, we will be blown away by the number of friends we will receive and, possibly more importantly, by the friends we have had all along but just couldn't see.

Because at the heart of the matter, she is enough and so is her momma.

2Corinthians 12:9 Ephesians 2:8 Ephesians 2:13 Isaiah 43:4

I'll Do It Myself

My mantra for my entire life has been, "Never mind. I'll do it myself."

It was the only way I could live life and feel safe. There were so many promises made and unfulfilled, that I began to stop trusting anyone's words, and definitely their actions.

I refused to be vulnerable because it hurt too much to suffer constant disappointment. I pulled away from the world, and decided that I would handle everything that came my way simply on my own.

As the eldest of five kids in an alcoholic home I became the family hero, and it was my job to protect my siblings the best way I could from the rage of my dad. I didn't ask for this title, nor did my parents sit me down and tell me that this was my place in our family.

I took this role on all by myself, and began to perfect the profession of care taking throughout my growing up years.

I cared for others. I cared for them to the point that they never needed to learn to care for themselves. I needed to be indispensable. I needed to be needed. It was my identity.

Today I am looking at how I've lived my life. What were my motives? How have my behaviors helped others? More importantly, how have my behaviors helped me? Has my life been enriched because of all I have given and continue to give?

In some cases absolutely my life has been blessed. But when it came to taking care of someone when I should have been letting them learn to care for themselves, we all suffered.

Here I am today feeling tired and bruised. I'm in pain and now I need to decide if I am willing to let down my walls of security and be totally vulnerable. To tell people I need them. To open myself up to let others care for me.

What if I ask for help and you say no? What if I seek your help and you ignore my pleas? What if I put myself on the line and you walk away?

That's the lie. Right there. In my face. Fear of being abandoned, again.

The truth is that when I let go, when I drop the brick wall I have secured around my heart, when I tell you that I need your help....

I open the way for you to walk towards me, take my hand and not only care for me but love me in the process of my healing.

Psalm 56:3 Psalm 143:8 1John 5:14 Hebrews 13:6

Heart Rhythms

As I look back over my life I see a timeline that looks a bit like a heart monitoring machine.

I've never been in a room of someone I love watching a machine communicate what the heart of a human being is doing.

But I do know that when the monitor shows a flat line, the heart has stopped and life has ended.

How many times have I cried out to God asking Him to let my life be easier, to make my challenges less complicated, and to smooth everything out evenly?

Or screamed at the top of my lungs, "Take this Father. I can't do this anymore."

And then I think of the heart machine.

Oh there have been many moments where I've been in a emotional arrhythmia and my timeline looks like an earthquake monitor that's gone completely berserk.

The extremes of my ups and downs seem unbearable at the time.

But the indication is that I have a life I'm living with courage and I'm in the middle of it every day.

When the arrhythmia happens I know I need to ask for help.

Like the nurses who run to a code blue and use the paddles to jolt a person's heart back into a healthy rhythm, I go to God and ask Him to help me slow down, reboot, refocus and trust His plan.

Daily I seek His counsel and wisdom.

I pray for a quiet spirit of discernment.

I pray for a forgiving heart that loves openly and freely.

I pray for compassion for myself and others.

And most of all I come back to that space of gratitude.

I am alive and my heart beats with every breath I take.

My rhythms represent that, although there may be times when my emotional state is totally out of whack, at th9ose times I have a God who I can go to who will bring me back to center.

I no longer hunger for a smooth flat line of easy.

Instead I give 100% of myself to the precious life I have, living wholeheartedly with a faithful spirit.

I take life one step at a time allowing the natural flow of outcomes to become known.

I breathe in and out with confidence that I am in the right place at the right time to learn the lessons I need.

And I welcome the unpredictable life rhythms that speak to my heart with the whisper of God, "I have you in the palm of My hand. Relax and let go. I've got this one and you are safe in my care."

Deuteronomy 31:6 Isaiah 41:10 Psalm 20:1 Psalm 46:1

Goals

So I woke up this morning with this prayer:

"Dear God, I have big Mary Kay goals this month. I'd like 6 new qualified team members.

Amen."

This was God's quiet response as I sat in silence.

"Whoa! Hold on a minute.

I love that you are focused on your goals, and you want to include Me but I think you may need to pray a bit differently on this.

Sometimes, Susan, I get the feeling you think of me like Santa Claus.

You've been good, done what you should, so now I give you what you want simply because you've asked.

There is so much more to what I want for you and my question is this, 'How many people's lives will you touch in My name today?'

Goals are important.

Focus is important.

Passion is important.

But it depends on where those things are rooted.

If they are rooted in Me, for Me and to bring honor to Me, then I'm all for it.

However if the motives are ego driven, there may be a problem.

Truly I want to give you your heart's desires and in order to do that, those yearnings must be aligned with what my will is for you.

If they aren't, you may not see the results you're asking for.

If that's the case, I urge you to be in prayer and surrender your disappointments to Me.

I am working on your behalf and for your good. ALL the time.

So go about your day and look for my blessings in unexpected places.

It will be in those moments of trusted surrender that you will find Me and be delighted in the surprises, for My gifts are everywhere.

I will be watchful as you continue to discover how deep My love for you is and I'll share in your smiles as you find Me in your daily life.

Be blessed my child. Be oh so blessed."

Psalm 127:1 Proverbs 15:22 Proverbs 16:9 Proverbs 19:21

Saying No

How many times have I heard that saying "NO is a complete sentence."

And that my no doesn't need an explanation, a defense, an argument or justification.

It is just no.

As a codependent who has been working a lifetime on setting boundaries and sticking to them, the word no was almost impossible to utter from my lips.

I think I was programmed to say yes.

I nodded my head in agreement when everything inside me screamed to shake my head no.

I said what I didn't want to say to avoid confrontation, disappointing someone or causing another to feel anger towards me.

And the result was I resented the hell out of them and hated myself for not being honest.

When I finally understood that it was vital to my emotional health to use the no word, I flew to the opposite side of the spectrum and wanted to say no to everyone, for everything, all the time.

I was still scared that if I didn't accept your offer, I would never be given the opportunity again to say yes.

But that was where trusting came in.

Trusting in God.

Trusting in me.

Today I'm learning to take time to respond.

To pray about what I need to do, and what God is asking of me.

To be mindful in my responses.

To be proactive in the decision making rather than reactive.

It's okay today to tell a friend I need 24 hours before I give my answer.

Let me think about it and I'll get back to you.

When I give myself permission to go quiet, to shut out the voices of my past that scream those old fears in my ears, I can be safe in knowing that when I give you my answer it will be MY answer.

I will feel confident, steady and sure of myself when I tell you no.

I will say it with kindness and respect.

I will also let it be a complete sentence.

And I will smile to myself for how far I have come.

Colossians 4:6 Matthew 5:37 Philippians 4:8 James 5:12

I Don't Understand

It began yesterday with a simple phone call my husband made to dear friends on the east coast.

Joe is great at staying connected to others, and these friends have been in his life since high school.

I was in the back room doing my exercises and could hear him laughing in his office in between sentences.

Finishing his phone call, he walked back to where I was laying on the floor and smiled.

It must have been a good conversation I thought to myself.

But his talks with this friend always brings laughter and fun.

Joe shared with me how his friends had gone to a beautiful family gathering to attend their grandson's wedding. Everyone was there from both sides of the family and there was love and joy everywhere.

Then he proceeded to tell me they had just put their boat in the water on the Hudson River so they could begin to enjoy the upcoming summer.

In between bringing me up to date on their traveling and the boat mooring, Joe said, "Oh and by the way they're sorry about your dad."

Then he was on to how they are going to fly Southwest Air now instead of American.

Really?

These are friends who send Hanukah cards and I never got any kind of card saying they were sorry that my dad died.

I know. I get it. Expectations are premeditated resentments. But at this moment all I was feeling was hurt.

And then I got a message from a friend who decided not to support my Operation Sunscreen this year since she is giving in other places. She said thank you for understanding.

At that moment the little girl in me started to spin.

There were no words for her to communicate how out of control she was feeling.

I laid on the floor for a few more minutes before deciding what to do next.

The world was moving on at the speed of light, and all I could think of was that my dad is dead.

I had Bible study to go to, but had already sent word I wasn't going to show up. Besides I lost my study book and hadn't done my homework.

"Forget it," I thought as I almost got back in bed.

I grabbed a shake and sat down at the dining room table to join Joe for breakfast.

He looked at me and said, What's going on?"

I just sat there.

Finally I told him that the little girl inside me was angry. Hurt. Lost. Confused.

He reached out, covered my hand with his and whispered, "It's going to be alright."

All I wanted to do was snatch my hand away from his and be angry.

When my friend who wasn't helping with my fundraiser said "thank you for understanding" I wanted to scream! Don't thank me. I don't understand. I don't understand why you're not helping. I don't understand why seven of my friends have died in eight months or why my dad had a heart attack and is dead now. I don't understand why my mom has Alzheimer's.

I DON'T UNDERSTAND ANYTHING!

I simply bowed my head in front of my husband and went silent.

I was in such deep pain.

Already dressed in case Joe needed me to go with him to the senior center to help with the boxes of documents that were to be shred, I decided I'd head to Bible study with my Bible and my sorrow.

What better place to be.

The Thumpers (as my husband refers to our group) were surprised to see me as they all got the message I was going to be a no show.

Standing at the kitchen counter I spilled my song of woe and told them I was so angry.

One of my dear friends said, "I remember when my mom died and I wanted to look at everyone who was living their lives and say, "Don't you get it? My mom just died."

And then she looked with those precious eyes of hers and shared "The world doesn't stop when someone we love dies."

I silently gasped as I gulped down the tears that were going to explode.

She hit the nail on the head. How dare life move on when everything in me wants to stand still and grieve the loss of my daddy?

That's what life does. It moves on. Just like that.

So I held that small little child that lives deep inside me and soothed her pain while I sat with my Thumper girlfriends, and let them pour their love on me.

And you know what?

It ended up being a pretty darn good day.

Psalm 30:5 Ecclesiastes 7:2 Psalm 119:28 Job 2:11

I Don't Want to Play It Safe Anymore

That doesn't mean I want to run out on the freeway and dance like no one's watching. But it does mean that my comfort zone is getting too small, and I'm not comfortable in it any longer.

Does stepping out of my comfort zone make me want to throw up? Yep, just a little bit.

But I am exhausted from holding up the safety walls to keep danger out. When I desperately try to hold at bay the things that cause me fear, I am also holding back the things that bring me joy.

I know I will carry regrets with me if I don't jump out and live my life with more abandon, faith and excitement.

And seriously, what have I been afraid of all these years? I believe it's the power I've had all along that I just kept giving away.

It was safer to be a victim than to be so victorious that the world would stand up and take notice!

My light needs to shine just like yours!!!

We all need to shine the light of God boldly and beautifully.

You BE you!
I'll BE me!!!
And we'll BE ENOUGH!

Matthew 5:16 John 12:35-37 Luke 11:34-35 Psalm 119:130

Change is Coming

I've always loved the East Coast because of the clearly defined seasons that part of the country experiences.

My dad's parents lived in North Carolina, and when we were little and could all fit in a station wagon, we would take road trips to visit them.

It was always in the summer time and the humidity was obnoxious. But as kids we were generally oblivious to the constant sweat dripping from our noses. We were just so busy playing in the red clay dirt with our cousins. We seriously drove my mom crazy with the stains that covered our clothes after a day of discovery in the local woods.

Those were great times and the only chances I had to enjoy the eastern part of the United States.

Until I married my husband, Joe.

Joe was born in Long Island, New York, and moved to California many years before I met him. But his heart lived in the city of New York where he had many years of meeting life head on as he grew into the man he is today.

For our honeymoon he took me to visit the city that never sleeps, and my heart fell in love all over again. Our time strolling down 5th Ave., going to the top of the World Trade Center, sight-seeing at the Statue of Liberty, and taking the ferry to Ellis Island sewed into my spirit a hunger for more. Not just for New York City, but for life experiences that I'd missed while I was raising my drug addicted children and moving from one marriage to the next trying not to drown in the chaos of my every day existence.

Trips to the east coast became more frequent, and six years ago I was delighted when we decided to take a road trip across the USA. That adventure changed me.

Forever.

I have always loved the seasons.

When I was 21 and newly married to my first husband, we moved to Butte, Montana. It was there that I began to fully experience life with seasons. We had a full year in what I believed was the coldest place on earth. I'd never heard of plugging your car into an electrical socket before you want to bed. But it didn't take me long to "Get it." It was freezing and there was snow. Lots of snow.

And there were seasons. Ice melting and flowers beginning to poke their heads up through the thawing ground. Summers with baseball games and Dairy Queen as the sun began to fade behind the mountains. Leaves changing colors and slowly lilting to the ground as they let go of the branches they called home. Soft snowflakes that fell peacefully outside the bay window as the fires burned inside the warm houses that lined the quaint and quiet streets.

Oh how my heart knew it was home. Living in a place where the seasons greeted me when I opened my front door filled me with a joy for life I'd never tasted before. It was like God was pouring His heart of love right into me. I was getting a love transfusion each time I stepped outside into His world. I was so hungry for His presence, and I each time I found myself in a space where the seasons lived, I vibrantly came alive.

In that place I was reminded that if God created the world to go through transformation each year, then He must have made me with the same plan in mind.

Where did I get the notion that I was designed to work, make it happen, get more, be more, have more, produce more and work more?

That was the lie I bought into each day as I got up and tried to figure out how to live a productive life.

And somewhere along the path of life I discovered something new and profound.

I am the seasons and as they changed, I changed too.

On our trip across country I, once again, was coming into a "fall" of my life and God was preparing me to shed the things that no longer served me. Ideas, beliefs, behaviors and patterns.

I sat quietly in our friend's home with coffee in hand and watched as the colors of the leaves went from vibrant greens to rich shades of crimson red, sunflower yellow and hot orange.

At the same time I felt my soul evolving into soft and subtle shades of kindness, compassion and understanding.

Each morning I was greeted with God's reminder that He is the designer of this incredibly majestic world and of my life. I need not worry, scurry or fear as the leaves of my life begin to fall at my feet. I need only trust the process of this great and glorious God.

I let go. I became still. I knew that winter was not far behind.

Winter was coming to steal the leaves from the boughs of the trees that had held them since they first bloomed in the spring. My own personal winter had arrived as well, to pluck my obsessive need for external accomplishments that had painted my life with defining colors of success and failure.

As the leaves dropped one by one to the frozen ground, the homes that were hidden behind those trees began to light up with warm amber lights shining through frosted window panes. A life that had been buried behind the thick forests, shared silent smoke signals letting me know that there was an unknown world ready to be seen.

Was I getting a glimpse of my new world?

Was there more for me than I could ever imagine?

If I was willing to release my need to control the lives of my children, my marriage, my business and my own life, let go of cars, and abandon old, stale and learned beliefs, would I begin to breathe more easily and see the new doors that were about to open?

The answer was YES!

I was being transformed and I knew it, felt it, believed it and trusted it.

God was helping me to live out the seasons of my life with more color and passion than I could ever have created on my own.

Change was coming. And I was thrilled.

A little nervous but nonetheless, excited and grateful to be here and to share my love for life with you.

What changes are you getting ready to experience? What old beliefs are you being prepared to let go of? What new and exciting doors are being opened for you? Are you willing to step through them and live your life OUT LOUD?

Remember that you are never alone, and that the world and the love of others are walking with you as you are led to a peace beyond your human understanding.

It's going to be quite a ride. Buckle up. The ride is about to begin.

2Corinthians 3:18 Philippians 1:6 Matthew 5:16 Colossians 3:10 Psalm 51:10

"Tending the Garden."

Tend, an interesting word. I looked up the definition and this is what I found: Predisposed to, prone, working toward.

Not exactly the message I was trying to convey when I used the word with garden.

My intention was to communicate more the idea of loving over, paying attention to, nurturing. You get the idea.

I never learned to tend to anything that was alive that might need my time and attention including my children. I am not proud that I was not a nurturer in any stretch of the imagination. I was more a "hatchet" kind of woman.

When it came to obstacles standing in my way, I would use my emotional hatchet to clear the way so I could simply move on to the next thing so quickly I didn't have time to feel any sense of loss. It's how I kept my heart intact and my mind occupied so there was no room for sadness or regret.

This is a classic case of "I couldn't give what I never got." I was in left field without a mitt and I was clueless.

I was unprepared to be a wife, mother or even a friend, and these are relationships that need tending.

What I was comfortable with was isolation so I could always feel safe. All that remained was pretending to be someone I wasn't.

Pretty. It's clean and beautiful with no flaws. That's what I wanted you to see when you looked at me.

Clean, beautiful and flawless. I worked hard at creating a look that would invite you to like me, but not necessarily to know me. A face that smiled even when I wanted to cry. A face that looked well kept when underneath there was sorrow and loss. There was so much I never wanted you to see, like the weeds that grew in my soul that were eating my spirit alive. Anger, resentment, hatred for those who hurt me. How could I let you into that dark place when all I could present was pretty?

Until I grew a garden...... and slowly began to understand.

How could I ever invite you to see my backyard garden when there might be unsightly weeds?

Why not just dig up the garden and start again? You would never see the mess that comes with growth, any kind of growth.

How many times have I done just that with things and people in my life? Confrontation? No way. Just move on and start over. Oops, another weed. Moving on, again and again.

Until I grew a garden.....

It all began with clearing a space. Cleaning the earth, sifting the good from the bad and preparing to plant. What would I plant? Just throw a bunch of seeds everywhere and pray for flowers, zucchini and tomatoes.

Oh, that's not how you do it? It takes more time than that? Well hurry up. I want pretty.

Not so fast was the message God kept giving me each time I stepped outside.

God quietly whispered, "Breathe Susan. Look around. What do you want to grow in this place?"

"I don't know God. What do you think I should grow here? I just want to do your will."

"Suze," He chuckled. " It's your garden and it really doesn't much matter to Me what you plant. What matters to Me is what you plant in the garden of your soul."

"So I can plant whatever I want and you're okay with it?"

"Yes." was God's reply.

"When it comes to this garden, that's exactly what I'm saying. But hear Me when I say that all gardening takes time and thought. You plant what you want to grow. And then you tend to those seeds. You nurture, water, talk to and encourage. If you plant tomatoes then you must except tomatoes. If you hope for carrots you will be disappointed. If you want beautiful flowers then you can't plant squash."

"Anything else?" I asked.

"Be mindful what you are sowing with your actions and thoughts."

"That sounds simple." I say.

'Yes, simple but not easy. It's your nature to want everything to happen right away, fast, now. But that's not how this process works. It takes time and more time. It requires you to think. What you sow you reap. If you sow seeds of anger and resentment, envy and spite, you will reap more of the same bitterness you planted."

God again pointed out, "Tending to your garden means taking time to weed out the things that no longer serve the needs of the plants. Weeds choke growth. When you are worried and obsessed, you stifle the development of peacefulness and gratitude. And plants, like people, grow at different rates of speed. Some just take longer than others to reach their full potential. I never intended that everything evolve at exactly the same timetable. "

"Do you understand?"

"I think so, God."

"Then go out and give your time and attention to the garden of My people. Tend to those who are needy, feed those who are hungry, nurture those who are parched and allow me to work through you. With your focused efforts and My plan WE can create miracles together."

2Corinthians 9:6 Luke 8:15 Luke 8:11 Galatians 6:8

"This or Something Better."

I don't know how many times I've heard this statement referenced when I was longing for something that may not have been in my best interest, and I don't think I cared whether God thought what I yearned for was best for me. All I know is that I wanted it, and I wanted it right now.

Whether it was a customer, friend, business partner or boyfriend, I have spent my whole life having temper tantrums when it came to not getting what I wanted.

If it was this or something better, you can bet it was THIS that I wanted. No negotiating. No reasoning things out. It didn't matter if the "this" made sense or not. I wanted THIS!!!! Period.

I never understood why I was so driven to choosing the things that didn't serve me well. Maybe it was simply the fact that I had to choose for myself. I was determined to prove that I had the power to make my own choices. I was claiming my independence, but at what cost?

Seriously, I look back at my behavior and wonder what was I thinking when it came to arguing with

God. Was I so incredibly demanding that I was fooled into believing I could really get Him to change his mind and reconsider my request? Was I so desperate for success and love that I continually settled for far less than second best? Couldn't I see that if I waited and trusted for just a little while longer that I might have received something far better than what I had hoped for?

I guess I just didn't think I was worthy of the best. After all, who did I think I was?

All I was sure of was that the agony I carried in the pit of my belly was too much to hold on to, and rather than sit with my pain and learn the lesson it was trying to teach me, I simply forged ahead to get something, anything to fill the emptiness. I was willing to settle for what was harmful rather than trust that God had a better plan.

Could that have been the shame I carried with me from childhood? The feeling of not being good enough, smart enough or pretty enough to allow the dreams I hid away in my soul to become my reality? Where did the feeling of not deserving come from? Was it the message my parents transferred to me because of their own bitterness of not getting what they had hoped for? Did they get the same message from their parents while growing up?

I wonder.....if we are all made in the image and likeness of God and we are all His wonderful and beautiful children, how did we ever arrive at a place where all we felt we deserved were the crumbs that fell from the banquet table?

Today I am coming to an understanding that it doesn't matter anymore where those feelings of unworthiness came from. Whether they took me hostage when I was a child or began to eat me alive when I was a young adult, today is all that matters. As I come to terms with my past beliefs and behaviors, in this moment I have a choice of whether I will believe the lies I was told or choose another belief system.

I no longer have to wrap the feelings of "shame" around me like a familiar and old warm blanket that felt like security from my past. I can open myself up to the possibility that the shame I've carried never belonged to me in the first place. I can shed that blanket of ugly comfort and surround myself with the kindness and comfort of God's love. I can begin today to believe that I am deserving of all things great and glorious, and I can stand firm in my convictions that the dreams planted in my heart were placed there by a God who thinks I am "ALL THAT."

So this or something better? I am all in for everything that's good, marvelous, wonderful and awesome because I deserve it.

How about you?

Psalm 147:3 Matthew 11:28 Isaiah 54:4 Psalm 69:19

Surrender

When I think of surrendering I think of quitting. Giving up. Waving the white flag and turning myself over to the enemy. Isn't that what we were taught in school when we studied our history lessons?

The battle fields of the young and old fighting for ideals and beliefs against others who feel the same way from their perspective.

People standing their ground with determination to win at any cost.

Growing up in an alcoholic home, my perception of the truth was often distorted and confused. I saw my home as a battlefield, and my abusive dad as the enemy.

For me, I was determined that I would never give in to him.

I was hell bent on standing my own ground.

But for what?

I learned later on in my life that there is no shame in giving in when the cost of winning is too high.

Even as a child I had deep convictions, and I knew what my dad was doing to his children was wrong and hurtful.

But to stand against him only made life more difficult and, at times, dangerous.

In that relationship I learned to fight authority.

To be angry when challenged.

To defend myself when accused of doing something I didn't do.

I would fight to the end and refused to give up.

There was no quit in me.

Today I understand that when I am called by God to surrender, it's for my own good.

God calls me daily to give up my will and my life over to His care.

To let go of the sword that I have carried my whole life in order to protect myself.

He is not the enemy.

He is my sword.

He is my protection.

So when I am on my knees each day seeking to understand the battlefields of life, I no longer have of fear giving in.

In my place of total surrender, I find God's grace and peace.

On what I used to call a battleground, I can now see as sacred ground.

And what I used to think of as giving up, I can now embrace as a giving in to a Father who loves me beyond words.

Today I willingly give Him my white flag and surrender my everything to Him.

My personal battle is over for God is fighting the battle for me.

Matthew 16: 24-25 Mark 10:28 Hebrews 11:6 Mark 8:35

The Fog

Him, her, them Fog.

It has never been about him or her or them.

It has always been my reaction to him, her or them.

Since I am aware of this, why do I find myself lost in the cold shadows again, desperately searching for a way out by putting on the fog lights and focusing outside of myself?

It doesn't work today, and it never worked then. If my eyes are on others then they're definitely not on God.

I'm clear on the fact that I can't change others, and on many days, can't change myself. The only option is to look to God for help.

Any time I am having a difficult time with where I am in my emotional, spiritual or physical life, it's generally because I have either lost my footing or I have lost my way.

I am angry, frustrated and feel helpless and powerless at the moment.

So I look over at you and start deciding what you should do with your life since it appears you definitely don't have it all together.

You are too something. Your pants are too tight. Your hair is too short. Your attitude is too abrupt. You're too skinny. Too rich. Too conceited.

Your behavior isn't to my liking. You aren't doing things the way I think they should be done. You're too loud. You're too quiet. Too messy. You are frustrating me. I can't see my part anywhere in this mess because it's all about you.

But what happens when I am searching out your flaws? I become oblivious to the fact that what I'm seeing when I look at you, is what I am seeing when I look at me.

Find the good in you, and I find the good in me.

But find the flaws in you, and that is all there is.

I want it to be all about you.

I want you to be the reason for my pain.

I want YOU to change.

If you change I'll be happy.

That is the lie I've believed my whole life.

I would be better today if my parents weren't so dysfunctional.

I would have a better job if my teachers had given me better grades.

I'd have a healthier marriage if the man I married would just own up to his misbehaviors and make some positive changes.

Please change so I don't have too.

It not only takes effort to make changes but, more importantly, it take willingness.

The willingness to see how my own stuff is playing a huge and primal part in what is going on in my life internally and externally.

When I am hurting, I often forget to seek God's help. I think it may be because there is a subliminal payoff for me to stay in a place of discomfort. It's familiar. It's easy to be in my comfortable place of victimization.

I was abused by my parents, so pain is what I know. I have grown accustomed to these feelings and, without being conscious of it, I go about recreating situations that will bring about the same results, the same feelings, and the same frustrations.

Until I have honestly and truthfully recognized that I am sick and tired of being sick and tired, I will stay put and blame you.

It takes downright courage to stand up and make changes.

It takes effort to find ways to be better.

It takes the willingness to be vulnerable to others, and to ask for help.

It takes a fall to my knees in surrender moment. And then another one and another one.

Letting go of the fog that keeps me safe in a comfortable place of uncomfortable requires that I hurt for as long as necessary until I can't take it anymore, and then I will do what is absolutely necessary to stop the pain.

And it's the same with those I love.

I cannot buy the heartache out of those I care so deeply about. I cannot demand they make changes because what they are doing is hurting me.

I can't shame them, blame them or guilt them into making long term change. When they are ready, they will do whatever they must to bring about their own surrender and inner quiet. I also understand that day may never come.

I can only seek out God and allow Him to change me. And when that happens my actions will begin to change, my results will be altered and those around me may change, too.

When the dance changes, my partner either has to adjust or leave the dance. And that is only a choice that he can make.

On the other hand if my partner changes the steps to the dance we are currently in, I am given the same opportunity.

It is in making peace with my own heartache that I can learn to live a life rich with moments of joy and pain, not having the need to run away from myself and others.

When I am in the fog today, I am no longer in a hurry to push my way out. I think about what I would do if I were in a car and hit a patch of fog. I would slow down. I might pull over and be quiet for a while. I doubt I'd be able to see ahead clearly enough to find the end to the fog, so I'd have to surrender my plan to God in order to continue safely on my journey.

When I decide that I am going to make this trip happen right here, right now and put my foot on the gas pedal to force my way, the end result could be that I hurt myself and those along the path that I can't even see.

I really can say that I hate it when my heart hurts and when those I love hurt. I don't like not knowing what's going to happen. I want to see the road ahead with clarity. I want to understand.

But it is in my desperate need to know, I am consumed with the character defect of control, and I start to squeeze the life out of everything that comes in contact with me.

Letting go is the only answer to my fear.

Letting go of those I cherish.

Letting go of outcomes.

Letting go of the steering wheel of life.

Taking the hand of God, and allowing Him to take the lead.

We all have choices.

Just for today I will choose to relax in my faith that someone far greater than I has a handle on life, and I am okay right where I am.

Proverbs 3:5 Philippians 3:13-14 Philippians 4:6-7 John 14:27

RAW

We all have a story. We are all unique. There will be no one other than you that will live the life you have been given. It's yours and was designed just for you.

And it's time that we each tell our story in our own words to the world.

Have you ever wondered what it would be like to let the walls down from around your heart, step out from behind your fears and get real?

Have you ever thought about what it would feel like to really tell your truth without fear of judgment or ridicule? To use your voice for something you were passionate about, not caring what anyone thought or said?

Are you tired of living your life for others instead of living your own life?

I know how that feels. I have known for a long time, but I never took the risk to create a change. I have waited for others to make a way for me. But no more. Not now.

I hunger for your truth, your honesty, your authenticity.

I want to hear your voice. See your eyes. Watch you smile. I want to know you.

My world has never encouraged me to let you see into my soul. Instead, I have been taught that I am not enough. Not pretty enough, smart enough, skinny enough. Whatever enough. I have lived watching you. I have measured my successes and failures based on other's time tables, measuring sticks and definitions. I have compared my worst with your best, and have come up short every time.

I don't know about you, but I'm tired and I suspect you may be too.

We are interconnected. We were never meant to live life alone, but instead to weave our stories of hope and triumph together. But until we all grab a hold of our courage and stop pretending that we have it all together, no one will ever know who we are, what we love and the principles we stand for.

It's time. Today is that day.

Today it's time to step into the gifts God has so generously blessed us with and be real and RAW.

RAW- Real Authentic Women.

It's time to stop living in the shadows of our secrets for we are not defined by our mistakes. We are changed through them, and if no one knows our honest experiences, how can any of us grow in the light of our individual uniqueness and power?

It is in our weakness that we grow strong.

Come take a journey with me and open some doors you may have never even known were closed. Come along side your sisters and open up your secrets and sorrows so we can cherish one another as we begin to breathe deeply the truth of who we are and how we each matter to one another.

Let go of your shame. Stand up tall and let your voice be heard.

We want to hear you.

1Timothy 4:4 Romans 12:6-7 2Corinthians 5:17 Jeremiah 1:5

Life Advice- short and sweet

If I could give anyone "life advice" right now it would be this:

1. Don't wait until you're as old as I am to be brave. Be BRAVE now.
2. Trust your instincts, and say your prayers, too.
3. Don't be afraid to make mistakes and own up to them. We all make them. It's just that some are not willing to admit it.
4. Use your voice not to spew judgment or hatred, but rather to praise others for giving it their best. Find the good in everything and then share it with everyone.
5. Be authentic. There is no other human being like you. You were chosen to be here on this earth to make a difference. Your presence matters.
6. No one ever said you had to be perfect, and if they did they were lying. Being you is enough because you are ENOUGH!

7. Smile even when your heart is sad because, no matter what, if you look hard enough, you will find a reason to be grateful.
8. Feel others love. It's there waiting for you to open your heart.

Matthew 5:42 Proverbs 19:20 Proverbs 12:15 Ephesians 4:29

The Art of Receiving

I believe we are born with the ability to trust and receive.

Until we are told the opposite either by words or the actions of others.

In my life lessons, I have discovered that many of us who have been raised in abuse, be it physical, psychological, sexual or emotional, learn very quickly that trusting is not safe.

My parents were wounded people who carried the scars of abuse from their childhoods.

They were not prepared to be my mom and dad and thus were not able to give me what they did not have.

I know and understand that today.

But many years ago I looked up to them like they were God. But all they were able to do was feed, house, provide an education and be unpredictable without the ability to show love, so I intrinsically began to internalize their lack of love-giving as my fault.

When they were unable to hold me gently, look me in the eyes with love and kindness and reassure me that my world was a safe place to grow, I began to believe I was the problem. Maybe I had done something wrong, maybe I wasn't good enough, pretty enough or smart enough. Maybe if tried just a little bit harder then everything would feel right inside me.

Then came the thought that if my parents really couldn't love me, how would I ever trust that God could and would.

Thus began my journey of trying to please others in order to feel like I was worthy.

Care taking became who I was rather than what I did.

The relationships I gravitated to were with those who needed help or so I thought. They were the people who had no friends. They were the loners at school. They acted like they didn't need anyone and clearly felt unloved, unwanted and alone.

Susan to the rescue. Whether you asked for my help or not I was Johnny on the spot with my care and concern and if I had it my way I would lead you out of despair and right into the arms of God.

Me, the one who didn't trust God, and I was going to lead you there. Right!

What I didn't know was that at the deepest level of who I was lived the idea that if I could just fix those wounded people I fell in love with, then maybe the hole in my soul that kept crying out for love could be filled.

However an inside hole cannot be healed with an outside solution.

Hurt people hurt people, and in my neediness to fix you, I ended up hurting you and then let you victimize me.

What a painful cycle.

I looked for those who were good at taking, and emptied myself over and over again trying to feel deserving of love and belonging.

At some point, I became so physically and mentally exhausted that I didn't even know I was depleted and had nothing left to give.

That's when the darkness started to envelop me like a warm blanket of comfort.

In my head I knew this was a dangerous place to be moving towards, but my spirit was so tired, that I didn't have the strength to fight it.

However deep inside me I believed there was a God that would never let me go. He had His hand on me, and even when I couldn't feel Him, I knew He was there.

Slowly He began to breathe life back into me. And in my willingness to be quiet and still in those scariest of places, I started to feel His presence and hear His soft gentle voice giving me direction.

"Small baby steps," He would whisper.

"You're okay. I'm right here. I will never forsake you. You are my child and I love you."

"Inch by inch" I moved tirelessly toward God's love and care and began to emerge into His light of promise.

Gradually, and with trepidation, I began to allow God to pour His spirit of love and tenderness into me.

The hole was big and the well deep.

I had given so much of myself to others, I didn't know how to receive.

To even admit to another human being that I might need their assistance created such anxiety in me.

I was afraid they would say no if I asked, and then be filled with shame for being vulnerable enough to ask.

The idea of needing any living person in my life, after years of unmet promises and disappointments, left me feeling emotionally tortured just thinking about it.

So instead I protected myself from what I perceived as abandonment and harm by pushing the world away and carrying the hidden mantra of "I can do it myself."

Rather than needing you, I made it my business to create an environment where you needed me.

And then I could be in charge.

But all I was really doing was shutting out love and living in the illusion that I could control my life and those around me.

What a lonely life, and I was constantly on the verge of resenting everyone for everything. Until I opened myself to the idea that in God's eyes I was already worthy of being loved and cared for. I didn't have to earn it nor prove my value.

And when I was willing to drop my defensive walls and receive God's unconditional love and acceptance, then and only then could I begin to accept yours.

Psalm 143:6 2Corinthians 9:8 Matthew 5:6 Romans 8:32

A Conversation with God

I went outside earlier today to have my lunch under the big, beautiful shade tree in our backyard.

It was a warm day, my heart was feeling heavy, and I just needed some time alone with God. I have actually been feeling sad the last few days and don't know why.

It's at times like these that I recognize when I go desperately looking for answers to the "Why" question, it's generally my way of trying to get the feeling to stop. If I can understand why I have it, then I can control it and make it go away. NOT!

This is when I need to go quiet, be still and let the uncomfortable feeling be with me until it goes away. I don't like waiting for a painful feeling to dissapate. I want it gone right NOW!!!

As I sat there looking around the yard at the flowers we just planted and the new fence that gives us some much needed privacy, I saw a bunch of dried-up brown leaves gathered up against the furthest part of the back yard, not too far from where I was sitting having lunch.

What a mess back there, I thought to myself.

"Why don't you clean it up?" God said.

"What?" I mumbled. "It's not my job to clean up this mess. It's the gardener's job."

"Hm. Well since you're the one looking at it and you have some time, why don't you take a little while and rake up the leaves? And why not water the flowers that are really looking beautiful right now as well," God replied to my whining.

"Come on God. I just came out here to have lunch with you." I responded. "Besides, I have work to do."

"Work?" God questioned curiously.

"What work do you need to be doing right now that could be any better than feeding my plants and raking the dead leaves that are preventing my plants from breathing?" He continued.

"I'm supposed to be doing something BIG, like changing the world, in Your name of course." I said.

God smiled.

"Susan, I am the one who changes the world. You are my child, and it's not your responsibility to take care of anything other than what I am asking you to take care of. It's time for you to learn to relax and trust that I have everything under control. You don't have to try so hard anymore."

"Don't just do something. Sit there. But God that is one of the hardest things for me to do….be still. Aren't I supposed to be productive doing Your will?" I asked.

"All you need to do is BE. You were never meant to be a human doing, just a human being. It's really that simple, but I know it's not easy. It's almost impossible for my children to get this lesson."

"Why God?" I wondered out loud.

"Because you're human. It's your humanness that pulls you into the world calling you to do something. In my world, I ask for your time. Not all your time, just some of your time. There will always be enough hours in the day to get done what needs to get done. But I want time with you so I can pour my love and attention into you. So I can bring you peace in a crazy and hectic day. It's ME I want you to adore, not the goals of the world."

"I get it God. Please help me to learn this one. I want to slow down and hear your voice. I am hungry to know Your will for me, and I am so clear that I can't do it on my own." I pleaded. "I'm tired and sad and don't know why."

"Just rake the leaves and water the flowers." He suggested.

"But isn't that just what I'm supposed to stop doing, being busy?" I said.

"Only when it's your will that you are focusing on that keeps you away from Me. And you know exactly what I mean." God laughed, as He whispered His words to me.

He was right. I knew perfectly well what He was referring to. I have pushed my will for a long time and it never left me feeling fulfilled and complete.

So I grabbed the rake, the big green trash can and my husband's gloves and I went about doing God's work in the garden.

John 9:31 Romans 12:2 1Thessalonians 5:8 Deuteronomy 5:33 1John 2:17

The Sunset of Life

After getting up at 6:00 a.m., to be showered and dressed for my second physical therapy appointment at 7:00 I stopped in the kitchen, looked out into the dark of the morning and wondered what today might bring.

I knew I was going to visit my mom and dad four hours north of where I live.

It had been a couple weeks since I last saw them, my dad in his new studio apartment at the assisted living facility and my mom in the Alzheimer's care building on the same property.

It hadn't been that long ago when I was here with my sister placing mom in her new home for her first night alone. She didn't want to be there and when it was time for my sis and I to leave, she sat at the table in the dining room with her head hung and a quivering chin trying not to cry.

Dad had been in the hospital and mom couldn't be left alone any longer. Everything was happening so fast. And we knew that we all had to come together in agreement to find her a new and safe place to live.

But the plan was never for them to stay at this facility long term. They were going to move to Washington state where my daughter Katie (who is a registered nurse specializing in geriatric care) would watch over them in their new place, Sherwood Village.

They would be able to live in the same apartment at this new skilled nursing home and not be separated like they were in Santa Maria. And up north my mom and dad would he surrounded with young family, their two oldest grandchildren, five great grandchildren and my ex-husband they love and adore.

However, today we were in the process of going through their home of ten years and eliminating what was not needed, setting aside what they would take and leaving the rest to be sold in an estate sale.

I arrived at my dad's apartment about 3:00 pm and was completely exhausted. Not just from the drive, but from everything else that was swirling around my life, including my chronic back pain, their transition, Joe's eye surgery and knee replacement, along with his recuperation period following those surgeries.

It was not an easy time and yet I was truly grateful for the opportunities I had to be there at every turn with those I loved.

I walked slowly to my dad's room to find the door ajar and quietly knocked as I let myself in.

He was laying on his bed but awake.

I announced myself and intended to sit next to him. Instead I just let myself give in to my exhaustion and gently laid down beside him. He put his arm around me and said, "You're tired? Why don't you rest and take a nap?"

My dad was never a nurturer. He couldn't see through his rage. But somewhere in my childhood there were glimpses of kindness that showed up unexpectedly weaved in and out of his angry outbursts.

And although he was the primary abuser in my life, I never doubted that he loved me.

I was touched by his gentleness when he suggested I take time to rest.

I wanted to surrender completely to my tiredness but I didn't have time. Instead I rolled over to look at him and we talked.

We talked about his having to give up his car, his feeling of losing his independence, his hurt and anger for being forced into a reality he never thought he would have to live.

It was a moment of tender mercy, kindness and forgiveness all wrapped up into a 10 minute discussion of the difficulties of growing older.

We both knew that being in this stage of life was not easy. Not for them or their children. We knew that if we all hung in there together, giving the best we could at every twist and turn, then we would survive this change and be better for it. Transition was coming, and we were all keenly aware there was nothing we could do to stop it.

I smiled at my dad, feeling grateful for this intimate moment we seldom shared.

And with that, he sat up and announced, "Let's go get your mom. I need a ride to Home Depot."

I laughed to myself and thought Yep......that's my dad!

Deuteronomy 31:6 Ecclesiastes 3:1 Jeremiah 29:11 Joshua 1:9

God is in the Details

I left Bible study in Corona to head to Costco for gas. Filled up and got back on the freeway as I had a makeover to do at 1:30 p.m.

On my way home I realized that I couldn't find my phone. I pulled over and looked EVERYWHERE for it.

Nope. No phone.

I MUST have my phone. Everything is in my phone.

Did I drop it at the gas station?

Dang it.

I got in my car and started the drive back to Corona all the while praying that God would send a phone call. If the phone rang in the car then that meant it was somewhere in my vehicle, and I could go home and find it.

Three miles in I got a call from my dearest and longtime friend Michele.

The phone rang in my car. YEEHAW!!!! WOOHOO!!!

I had it with me, but I just could not find it.

She said, "I don't know why I'm calling you. God just said call Susan. Is everything ok?"

And there HE goes again. Taking care of me just because I asked.

Thank you God.

How many times do I go to the frantic, out of control place before I stop and ask God for help?

Why do I make myself crazy when I know that God is right there listening and waiting for me to reach out?

I know why.

It's because when I was little and asked my parents for help, they asked me if I had done everything possible to accomplish the task before coming to them. My answer was always yes, and I was an emotional and frustrated mess by the time I gave in and finally went to them for assistance.

Today I am constantly reminded that God is in the details. I don't have to wait to ask for His help.

He is always there ready, willing and able.

Psalm 46:1 Proverbs 3:5-6 Matthew 7:7 1Chronicles 4:10

Good vs. Good

When I judge something as good, I do so with my feeble human understanding, which, by the way, is so incredibly limited.

I decide what is good, bad, right or wrong in my world. And it is based on the filters of my experiences.

But in God's world, who judges what is good?

And how do we come to terms with what we see as something that violates our mind set and registers as bad?

If life doesn't go my way or I don't get the results I want, do I scream out to the Almighty, "how could you let this bad thing happen?"

Do I shout from the mountain tops that my God is great only when my human desires are met in accordance to MY will?

I am so small in my human understanding of what is good and bad in God's domain.

What if it's all good?

What if it is good vs. good?

I am certainly not suggesting that evil is not alive and well in our world, and that things don't happen that can only be interpreted as bad by our human mind.

But what if we could go beyond our own judgment?

What if there was another way of understanding without labeling?

I'm not sure that in my own brokenness I could ever fully wrap my arms or heart around the total concept that God truly works everything out for the good for those who believe.

If God is like my puppet who can be manipulated to perform for me what I think I want and need, how can I believe in the magnitude of His magnificence?

I can't because I am playing God.

I will never understand God's ways, His will, His deep love for me.

I will completely understand that what I see as bad could be used for good to glorify God.

And can I totally surrender to the idea that God is good all the time?

ALL THE TIME?

Can I trust in Him completely when I have questions about the outcome of my prayers?

Can I believe in Him even in His silence?

Can I willingly surrender my need to judge Him when I'm angry and frustrated that He didn't answer my pleas in my way?

Can I still see God as good when I have determined that what has happened in my life seems so bad?

Those are big questions.

Deep and thought provoking.

If I'm open to being still in my moments of darkness and emotional confusion will the fog lift so I can embrace God for who He wants to be in my life?

A loving, kind, caring, Father who loves me beyond my human ability to understand?

And will I ever be able to say God is Good ALL the time?

I believe I will, and in this life long journey yearning to experience the whole of God's grace I will continue to grapple with a human mind seeking God's heart.

Psalm 143:10 1Timothy 4:4 Psalm 145:9 Psalm 100:5

Father's Day Without a Dad.

Father's Day looms ahead, and this year I will not have an earthy dad to celebrate. There will be no trips to Washington to surprise him, or phone calls that delight in the sound of his voice when he calls me "Sue Sue Baby."

There will be no cards mailed, no face time with my mom talking over him in the background. There will be no "I love yous" as I say goodbye. It will still be Sunday, but it will never be the same.

I knew that one day I might face this moment, but I hoped it would never come.

I think you know what I mean. We know life will end one day for all of us. We are running for the finish line, whatever that looks like, but we never really believe that we will stand in that reality until the day comes and smacks us right into the reality of loss.

Nothing is the same since my dad died. And yet everything is the same.

I'm still a mom and wife. Business woman and daughter. Grandma and friend.

I still live in the same house with the same phone number, and I have pretty much the same routines I had before April 17th.

I live 1300 miles away from where my dad was living and where my mom still lives.

But there is a hole in my heart that nothing can fill. A wound in my soul that no doctor or surgery can heal. Not a piece of chocolate cake, a new dress or pair of shoes, moose tracks ice cream or even a hug from those I love.

Those may soothe the pain for a moment, but nothing will take away the loss of a dad.

I know God loves me and has surrounded me with those who have walked this road before me. They are my village. They face their sorrow every day, and show me that it's okay to be quiet, stop the merry-go-round of life for a bit, sleep when I need to, and cry as often as the tears beg to be shed.

They are brave, courageous and generous with their experiences and memories.

I understand the day will come when I will help another when loss hits their soul and breaks their heart. I will become a part of their new village.

And even though the pain cannot be stopped, I can learn to live with that empty space that was created when my father left.

SO.....

Just for today I will remember.

Just for today I will be grateful.

Just for today I will walk a little more softly.

Just for today I will breathe a little more easily.

Just for today I will know that my dad is with God, and he delights in what he sees.

Psalm 62:8 Psalm 147:3 Psalm 34:18-19 John 16:22

Prayer

I sat in my quiet place this morning and reflected back on my life of prayer and what it has looked like.

For a long time it was a child's prayer.

"God, can I have a horse when I die and go to heaven?"

Amen

P.S. It's me, Susan

Then it became a prayer of a teenager that went like this:

"Dear God, my parents are driving me crazy. They don't get me. They'll never understand. Do something!!!!!

Can you please tell them it's ok if I use the car this weekend? I promise I'll be careful!"

Amen

As a young married woman who was pregnant:

"Dear God, please let me have a healthy baby and the resources I need to care for this baby. I'm scared to death."

Amen

Never will I forget those prayers at night for my children who seemed lost in a world of uncertainty and pain.

On my knees in those dark nights I cried out to God.

"Father I am desperate to know my child is alright. Please let me know you are there and they are okay. I have no idea where they are and if they are safe. Please Father send me a sign they are alive."

Amen

Now, at this stage of my life my prayers are more about God's WILL for me rather than what I think I want and am desperate to have.

Father,

As I sit reflecting on all the prayers you have answered I can't help but rejoice in Your miracles.

I feel Your presence here and know that You are the Conductor of the orchestra of life.

Sometimes I hear the clang of the symbols welcoming a huge miracle and other times when there is a lull in the music, I strain to hear the barely audible sound of the far off bell signaling that there is more to come....

I wait.

I listen.

I pray.

I believe.

And Father I seek Your will and beseech YOU in my continuous prayers for the answers.

I will hold steady as I trust you in ALL things.

And I honor and praise you in the name of Your Son, Jesus.

Amen

Prayers answered. Anxiety lifted. Rejoice.

Until the next time when I sent a desperate plea to our Father to spare the life of my dad and heal his earthly body so he could live and care for my mom.

Wait.

The answer came.

The answer was No.

My dad died.

Rejoice?

Not at first.

Sorrow, tears and anger.

Questions...

Why God? Why?

And then a I received a peace that overtook me as I saw that God was sparing my father months of ongoing suffering and also maybe answering my dad's prayer of "I'm so tired. Take me home."

How many times have I wondered why?

Questioned the waiting time. Happy for the rejoicing times, only to, once again, be brought back to the waiting?

Too many times to count.

Isn't it really about patience?

Rejoicing with God.

Waiting on God.

The older I get, the more I come to terms with the fact that God loves me beyond my ability to understand. The depth of his care is immeasurable, and cannot be described in human terms.

My ability to wait patiently may always be a struggle, for I am human and want what I want, when I want it.

But slowly the magnificence of God seeps from the knowledge I hold in my head to the love I seek in my heart.

And when His love rests in my heart and soul, in those quiet moments when I am totally surrendered....

I Get It.

I Feel Him.

I Know Him

I Receive Him.

GOD.

My Papa.

My Father.

And I rejoice!

1 John 5:14-15 Ephesians 1:18 Jeremiah 29:12 Romans 12:12

Change is Coming

I've always loved the East Coast because of the clearly defined seasons that part of the country experiences.

My dad's parents lived in North Carolina, and when we were little and could all fit in a station wagon, we would take road trips to visit them.

It was always in the summer time and the humidity was obnoxious. But as kids we were generally oblivious to the constant sweat dripping from our noses. We were just so busy playing in the red clay dirt with our cousins. We seriously drove my mom crazy with the stains that covered our clothes after a day of discovery in the local woods.

Those were great times and the only chances I had to enjoy the eastern part of the United States.

Until I married my husband, Joe.

Joe was born in Long Island, New York, and moved to California many years before I met him. But his heart lived in the city of New York where he had many years of meeting life head on as he grew into the man he is today.

For our honeymoon he took me to visit the city that never sleeps, and my heart fell in love all over again. Our time strolling down 5th Ave., going to the top of the World Trade Center, sight-seeing at the Statue of Liberty, and taking the ferry to Ellis Island sewed into my spirit a hunger for more. Not just for New York City, but for life experiences that I'd missed while I was raising my drug addicted children and moving from one marriage to the next trying not to drown in the chaos of my every day existence.

Trips to the east coast became more frequent, and six years ago I was delighted when we decided to take a road trip across the USA. That adventure changed me.

Forever.

I have always loved the seasons.

When I was 21 and newly married to my first husband, we moved to Butte, Montana. It was there that I began to fully experience life with seasons. We had a full year in what I believed was the coldest place on earth. I'd never heard of plugging your car into an electrical socket before you want to bed. But it didn't take me long to "Get it." It was freezing and there was snow. Lots of snow.

And there were seasons. Ice melting and flowers beginning to poke their heads up through the thawing ground. Summers with baseball games and Dairy Queen as the sun began to fade behind the mountains. Leaves changing colors and slowly lilting to the ground as they let go of the branches they called home. Soft snowflakes that fell peacefully outside the bay window as the fires burned inside the warm houses that lined the quaint and quiet streets.

Oh how my heart knew it was home. Living in a place where the seasons greeted me when I opened my front door filled me with a joy for life I'd never tasted before. It was like God was pouring His heart of love right into me. I was getting a love transfusion each time I stepped outside into His world. I was so hungry for His presence, and I each time I found myself in a space where the seasons lived, I vibrantly came alive.

In that place I was reminded that if God created the world to go through transformation each year, then He must have made me with the same plan in mind.

Where did I get the notion that I was designed to work, make it happen, get more, be more, have more, produce more and work more?

That was the lie I bought into each day as I got up and tried to figure out how to live a productive life.

And somewhere along the path of life I discovered something new and profound.

I am the seasons and as they changed, I changed too.

On our trip across country I, once again, was coming into a "fall" of my life and God was preparing me to shed the things that no longer served me. Ideas, beliefs, behaviors and patterns.

I sat quietly in our friend's home with coffee in hand and watched as the colors of the leaves went from vibrant greens to rich shades of crimson red, sunflower yellow and hot orange.

At the same time I felt my soul evolving into soft and subtle shades of kindness, compassion and understanding.

Each morning I was greeted with God's reminder that He is the designer of this incredibly majestic world and of my life. I need not worry, scurry or fear as the leaves of my life begin to fall at my feet. I need only trust the process of this great and glorious God.

I let go. I became still. I knew that winter was not far behind.

Winter was coming to steal the leaves from the boughs of the trees that had held them since they first bloomed in the spring. My own personal winter had arrived as well, to pluck my obsessive need for external accomplishments that had painted my life with defining colors of success and failure.

As the leaves dropped one by one to the frozen ground, the homes that were hidden behind those trees began to light up with warm amber lights shining through frosted window panes. A life that had been buried behind the thick forests, shared silent smoke signals letting me know that there was an unknown world ready to be seen.

Was I getting a glimpse of my new world?

Was there more for me than I could ever imagine?

If I was willing to release my need to control the lives of my children, my marriage, my business and my own life, let go of cars, and abandon old, stale and learned beliefs, would I begin to breathe more easily and see the new doors that were about to open?

The answer was YES!

I was being transformed and I knew it, felt it, believed it and trusted it.

God was helping me to live out the seasons of my life with more color and passion than I could ever have created on my own.

Change was coming. And I was thrilled.

A little nervous but nonetheless, excited and grateful to be here and to share my love for life with you.

What changes are you getting ready to experience? What old beliefs are you being prepared to let go of? What new and exciting doors are being opened for you? Are you willing to step through them and live your life OUT LOUD?

Remember that you are never alone, and that the world and the love of others are walking with you as you are led to a peace beyond your human understanding.

It's going to be quite a ride. Buckle up. The ride is about to begin.

2Corinthians 3:18 Philippians 1:6 Colossians 3:10 Psalm 51:10

11716177R00113

Made in the USA
Middletown, DE
21 November 2018